MW00441488

Other Books by Linda Wommack:

Colorado Gambling, The Early Years

Cripple Creek Tailings

Colorado History for Kids

From the Grave; Colorado's Pioneer Cemeteries

Our Ladies of the Tenderloin, Colorado's Legends in Lace

Colorado's Landmark Hotels

Colorado's Historic Mansions and Castles

Murder in the Mile High City; The First Hundred Years

Ann Bassett, Colorado's Cattle Queen

Haunted History of Cripple Creek and Teller County

CRIPPLE CREEK

BOB WOMACK

AND

THE GREATEST
GOLD CAMP ON EARTH

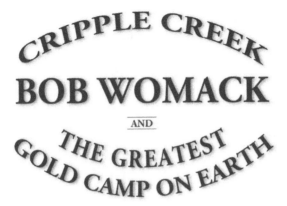

CRIPPLE CREEK
BOB WOMACK
AND
THE GREATEST GOLD CAMP ON EARTH

Linda Wommack

East of the Mountains  and West of the Sun

RHYOLITE PRESS, LLC
Colorado Springs, Colorado

Published in the United States of America by Rhyolite Press LLC
P.O. Box 60144
Colorado Springs, Colorado 80960
www.rhyolitepress.com

Wommack, Linda R.

CRIPPLE CREEK, BOB WOMACK
AND THE GREATEST GOLD CAMP ON EARTH
1st edition: June, 2019

Library of Congress Control Number: 2019905860

ISBN# 978-1-943829-20-0

PRINTED IN THE UNITED STATES OF AMERICA

Cover design, book design/layout by Donald R. Kallaus and Suzanne Schorsch
Cover photo: Denver Public Library, Western History Department, X-832. F-22733

$\mathcal{A}$ simple man with simple values, Bob Womack proved his simple gold theory, and "The World's Greatest Gold Camp" was born.

Dedicated to the memory of Robert Miller "Bob" Womack. A man who had the vision and tenacity to follow his dream.

And to my parents, Clovis Daniel Wommack, who encouraged my love of history, and Joyce Darlene Hoglund Wommack, who spent her life documenting the family genealogy.

And finally, to my late uncle, Curtis Haun Wommack: A Wommack legend in his own right.

CONTENTS

Foreword

Cripple Creek boasted of being "The Greatest Gold Camp on Earth." Unlike so much local bragging of being the world's first, greatest, best, tallest, etc., this claim actually approaches the truth. Indeed, for the first decade of the 20th century, Cripple Creek led the world in gold production.

In 1890, Colorado's last great mining bonanza occurred on the southwest side of Pikes Peak. At first, no one believed that Bob Womack had really found gold. Six months later a few men came to believe and joined Womack in forming the Cripple Creek Mining District.

Linda Wommack, (with a double m) great-great grandniece of the gold discover Robert Miller (Bob) Womack, has written a much-needed updated history of the "Greatest Gold Camp on Earth." Linda tells the tale through the eyes of Bob Womack, bringing him and Cripple Creek back to life. She takes us back to that auriferous era when the Cripple Creek payoff peaked by 1900. This bonanza helped pull Colorado out of the silver crash of 1893, perking up not only Colorado but the entire nation. While Womack sold out early, men like Winfield Scott Stratton, Spencer Penrose, Charles Tutt, Sam Strong, James Burns, and James

Doyle became golden millionaires.

In the first decade following Womack's initial 1890 strike, $65 million in gold shined global attention on Colorado. The six square mile Cripple Creek Mining District included ten mining camps and a population that boasted fifty thousand in 1900. The boomtown of Cripple Creek evolved from a small mining camp to a bustling city. Through it all, Bob Womack watched the growth, the arrival of the railroads, the devastating fires of 1896, and the bloody labor wars. After the 1903-04 Western Federation of Miners strike, Cripple Creek began declining. Mine owners who refused to share much of the wealth with their workers contributed to the blame. Cripple Creek is booming once again with new mining technology in the old diggings, updating this golden tale.

I have known Linda Wommack since 1993 and know her research to be top-notch. Through family documents, interviews with family members, and hours of museum, library and newspaper research, Linda has provided the reader with a wonderful history of the "Greatest Gold Camp on Earth." I have had the pleasure of working with Linda on various projects including bar tours, history talks, cemetery tours and excursions over the years. She is very passionate about Colorado history and this, her twelveth book on the subject, is Wommack's work at its finest.

Dr. Thomas J. Noel
Colorado State Historian
Professor of History at the University of Colorado Denver
Dr. Noel is the author or co-author of 53 books on Colorado.

A longtime former Sunday columnist for the Rocky Mountain News and The Denver Post, he appears regularly as "Dr. Colorado" on Channel 9's Colorado and Company.

Preface

On the south side of Pikes Peak, America's Mountain, lies the legendary mining mountain town of Cripple Creek. Men have passed through the region for centuries: the Spanish explorers, French and American trappers and traders, path finders, homesteaders and ranchers, and finally those eager men frantically searching for gold.

Traces of gold were found here and there over a period of several decades, but not much to speak of. Strange color in the rock that no one could identify and false rumors, even a hoax or two, but no real gold strike. That is until October 1890. Bob Womack filed the first substantial gold claim in the region and soon others followed. The Jimmies, Burns and Doyle, would make millions with the discovery of the Portland, and Winfield Scott Stratton would become the mining district's first millionaire when he sold his Independence for a cool ten million dollars.

Businessmen made their fortunes, too: men like Charles Tutt and Spencer Penrose, who financed his Broadmoor Hotel with the millions he made from the C.O.D. Mine. Albert E. Carlton, freighter, shipper, trader, and financier, only got richer when he built the Carlton Mill.

The mines of the Cripple Creek Mining District were the richest in the world. A vug of near solid gold was found twelve feet down in an otherwise normal hole in the ground. Named the Cresson Mine, it would eventually produce over fifty million dollars in gold. And there were more: the Elkton, Vindicator, El Paso, Anaconda, Jack Pot, and Gold King, just to name a few.

By the turn-of-the-century, the Cripple Creek Mining District was producing an average of $20,000,000 worth of gold a year. Other American mining districts of the era weren't even close. Alaska's Klondike region produced less than half that amount. Nevada's Comstock Lode only averaged $380,000 annually. Worldwide, Cripple Creek's only competition was South Africa's Witwatersrand discovery, which only yielded a third of the world's gold supply.

So rich were the mines of the Cripple Creek region that the gold production ended the national economic depression of 1893. One hundred years later, mining continues. Now, as then, it boosts the economy of the area.

And it all started back in 1890 by a man named Bob Womack. You might have heard of him. He's known as the founder of Cripple Creek.

Acknowledgments

I would first like thank my parents, Clovis D. and Joyce D. Wommack, for opening the world of history to me. I inherited my passion for history from my father. From my mother, I learned about my family's history through her decades of genealogy research.

I remember two particular research trips with my parents. My mother had finally discovered that our relative, Robert "Bob" Miller Womack, was buried in the Evergreen Cemetery. Early on a Saturday morning, we took a family drive to Evergreen, Colorado, and a visit to the cemetery. My mother was dumb-founded when she was told there was no burial record of a Robert "Bob" Miller Womack. It was sometime later, I don't remember exactly how long, that my mother discovered that, while Bob Womack was indeed buried in the Evergreen Cemetery, the cemetery was not in the town of Evergreen, but in Colorado Springs. This time we took a Sunday drive to the Evergreen Cemetery in Colorado Springs. Perhaps because it was an early Sunday morning, there was no one at the cemetery. My father finally found a caretaker who would show us where the Womack family plot was.

During our walk to the gravesite, which was at the other side of the cemetery, my mother asked the caretaker all sorts of questions. At the Womack family plot, my mother meticulously wrote down every inscription on every tombstone and foot stone, and then drew the entire plot layout, complete with the small white stone wall surrounding it, the trees and the shrubs. While she was doing this, my father was taking pictures of the tombstones and chatting with the caretaker. Then my mother had a few more questions. The caretaker must have thought my mother was a reporter or writer, with all of her questions. I was standing next to her and remember very distinctly what the caretaker said to my mother. "Bob Womack was not a drunk and don't you print otherwise."

Over the years, as I began to gather together my own research I remembered that caretaker and his final statement to my mother that day at the Evergreen Cemetery. Many secondary sources claimed that Robert "Bob" Miller Womack was indeed a drunk. As I read through each one of these books, it soon became apparent that Bob's alleged "drunkenness" began with a popular novel of the Cripple Creek region, published by Ballantine Pocket Books, in 1952. Astonishingly, the writers of the other books used this novel as a source and one in particular, wrote nearly word for word, accounts from the novel. In 1952, Marshall Sprague published Money Mountain: The story of Cripple Creek Gold. While many Cripple Creek historians consider this work a novel as well, it does contain footnotes and sources. However, Sprague writes that Womack took the "Keeley cure," developed by Dr. Leslie E. Keeley, and never drank again. Unfortunately, in this otherwise, heavily foot-noted work, there is no source cited for this claim.

As I continued with my research, I began to dispel myths and flush out the truth. I relied on experts in the history of Cripple Creek. My mother and I spent many hours with Cripple Creek historian and then curator of the Cripple Creek District Museum, Leland Feitz. I treasured my time with him and have relied on his informative letters he sent to me for this eventual work.

In 1989, my mother and I made several trips to Colorado Springs where we spent time in the Colorado Springs libraries, gathering information from prime sources including the Tutt Library resources, the local Womack genealogy information, and newspaper archives, available on microfilm. It was many hours of photocopying.

That same year, my mother and I also met with Leland Feitz and later, Erik Swanson, director of the Cripple Creek District Museum. His enthusiasm for the history of Cripple Creek and Bob Womack was a sheer delight. Swanson allowed us to go through the many shelves and boxes of documents, maps and photos. We returned a few more times over the next couple years, visiting with Swanson, copying source information, maps and purchasing photographs. On one of these trips, my mother presented Erik Swanson with a complete Womack/Wommack genealogical lineage, printed on fine parchment paper for his museum archives. I am indebted to Erik Swanson's help in my research and his friendship. Unfortunately, during a subsequent trip to the museum, shortly after Swanson's retirement, this generous gift from my mother could not be located. Thankfully, I still have my copy.

In 1992, during the Cripple Creek Centennial celebration, I had the privilege of being seated next to Cripple Creek's Historic Preservation Director, Brian Levine. Through his generous assistance, I was able to acquire more prime sources as well as maps and photographs. I am indebted to Levine's help as well as our continued friendship.

As with all research, I have relied on the ever-diligent work of friend, Coi E. Drummond-Gerhig, Digital Image Collection Administrator for the Denver Public Library. Not only did she provide nearly every photograph I requested, she also served up some real gems that I didn't know existed. My thanks to former Cripple Creek District Museum Director, Richard Tremayne, who always gave me access to the archives with a smile and a wave. Michelle Rozell, Director of Cripple

Creek's Heritage Tourism, was instrumental in helping me secure photographs of the region.

Finally, I would like to thank friends and family who provided support and encouragement. First on that list is my husband Frank, who helped to work out the research obstacles, and tolerated the many late nights of research and writing. Gayle Gresham, a dear friend has supported this endeavor from the beginning. She generously offered a photo of a painting of Bob Womack that has been in her husband's family for years.

Throughout the research and writing process, I relied on my dear friend, Connie Clayton. Her cogent comments, encouragement, and careful editing, strengthened this work immensely. I owe her my heartfelt gratitude.

Linda Wommack
December 16, 2017.

Introduction

Being a distant relative of Bob Womack, I get asked a lot of questions about Ol' Bob.

No, I didn't know him, he died in 1909, I was born some fifty years later.

No, I am not a direct descendant; Bob never married, and had no children.

Why is Bob's surname spelled with one M, while my surname is spelled with two M's? It was a common practice in the nineteen century to use different spellings of the surname to distinguish the many branches of the family. Bob's branch held to the original spelling, while my great-grandfather added an extra M.

But back to Bob.

As with any family history, there is a fair amount of exaggeration, legend and lore. In the case of Bob Womack's legend, there is no doubt, as history clearly records, that Robert "Bob" Miller Womack was the first to find high-grade gold in the Cripple Creek area which resulted in America's last great gold rush. Because of Bob Womack's rich gold find, over five hundred mines were discovered and worked during first half of the 20th century. Mining still goes on today.

This is the story of Robert "Bob" Miller Womack, the discoverer of Cripple Creek's gold, and the "Greatest Gold Camp on Earth."

Chapter 1

The Early Years

Bob's grandfather, John W. Womack, came west from his native state of Virginia, settling in Jackson County, Kentucky, in approximately 1810. There, he purchased land and engaged in farming. In 1813, the prosperous farmer took a wife. She was Phoebe Boone Bryan, the daughter of Mary Boone Bryan, a grand-niece of famed frontiersman, Daniel Boone. The two were married on September 27, 1813. Six years later, on December 8, 1819, their first child was born, Samuel Redd Womack.

As a child, Sam suffered from several ailments, all of which were minor and were probably due to allergies. In any case, Phoebe doted on the child. As he grew older, he attended school occasionally, depending on the the season, as his help was needed with the operation of the family farm. In 1842, twenty-three year old Sam married Corella A. Booker. The newlyweds soon started their own farm not far from Sam's father's spread. Children soon followed to this matrimonial union. Robert Miller was the first, born August 1844, Margaret in March 1846, Eliza in July 1848, and William in December 1851.[1]

Not long after the birth of his youngest child William, Sam took a keen interest in the enormous amount of gold being extracted from the American River in California, which had spawned the great western gold rush era in 1849. When Sam learned, in 1859, of the Pikes Peak gold rush in the Rocky Mountains, his interest sharpened. Perhaps Sam read glowing accounts in newspapers such as the following article, published in the *Missouri Republican*, dated March 17, 1859:

> "It is astonishing how rapidly we learn geography. A short time since, we hardly knew, and didn't care, whether the earthly elevation called Pike's [sic] Peak was in Kansas or Kamchatka. Indeed, ninety-nine out of every one hundred persons in the country did not know that there was such a topographical feature as Pike's Peak. Now they hear of nothing, dream of nothing, but Pike's Peak. It is the magnet to the mountains, toward which every body and everything is tending. It seems that every man, woman and child, who is going anywhere at all, is moving Pike's Peakward."

The Pikes Peak gold rush had caught the imagination of America, including Samuel Redd Womack. Four days after this article appeared, a reporter wrote of what he must have been watching for days. His piece was printed in the March 21, 1859, issue of the *Missouri Republican*:

> "Here they come, by every steamboat, hundreds of them, hundreds after hundreds from every place. Some have ox wagons, some have mules, but the greatest number are on foot, with their long-tailed blues, others in jeans with bob-tailed jockeys; in their roundabouts, slouch hats, caps and sacks. There are a few handcarts in the crowd. They form themselves into companies of ten, twenty, and as high as forty-five men have marched out, two-and-two, with a captain and a clerk, eight men to a handcart,

two at a time pulling the cart. Onward they move west, day after day, old and young, fat and slender, short and tall, handsome and ugly, the strong and the weak."

However, within months, the eastern papers were declaring the Pikes Peak gold rush as a "bust." This spawned the famous slogan, "Pikes Peak or Bust." The slogan was coined by the *Nebraska City News* in an article printed in the May 28, 1859, issue:

"Among the most significant mottoes we have seen upon any of the wagons going out to the mines, was that of an Illinoisan, about three weeks ago, inscribed in flowing letters of red chalk, though not in the most approved style of art —'Pike's [sic] Peak or bust.' The indefatigable and energetic sucker returned the other day upon a gaunt and starving mule, that looked as if he had climbed the peak. He was asked why he didn't go through. 'Wal.' he said, 'he'd got clean on beyond Kearney, and—he busted, so he just rubbed out 'Pike's Peak or bust,' and turned back."

It was during this time in 1859 that rumors of civil war were becoming more of a reality. Although Kentucky was a border state, it must have been after much discussion that Sam and Corella decided to leave the region. Bob, now seventeen years old, could be called upon to enlist in whichever side Kentucky decided to join, something his parents did not. Therefore it was decided that Sam and Bob would go to the Colorado gold fields, while Corella would stay behind with the younger children until, or if, something developed favorably out west.

Not long after the first shot was fired at Fort Sumter, in April 1861, Sam and Bob departed Kentucky. They traveled by train through St. Joseph, Missouri, and on to Atchison, Kansas. From there the two traveled by wagon following the South Platte Trail west, to the mining-supply town of Denver City.

After stocking up on supplies and food, Sam and Bob headed into the Rocky Mountains. They drove through the narrow Clear Creek Canyon, arriving at the gold camp of Payne's Bar. [2] George A. Jackson had found gold in the south fork of Clear Creek in May 1859. It was Jackson's find, along with the gold discovered at Gregory Gulch in January of the same year by John Gregory and William Greenberry Russell, that created the national movement westward, with the slogan, "Pikes Peak or Bust." [3]

Bob and his father found the area swarming with prospectors. Over fifty sluice boxes were lined along Clear Creek and near the mouth of Chicago Creek.[4] Horace A. W. Tabor had staked his first of many gold claims here the previous year, but had returned to Denver after the first snowfall. When Tabor returned in the spring of 1861, he found his claim had been jumped. Due to the vague mining laws at the time, Tabor had little recourse and simply left the area. It is possible, given the time frame, that the Womacks knew Tabor, although there is no record.

In any case, Sam Womack did not make the same mistake as Tabor had. Sam and Bob spent their time learning what they could of the mining prospects. Sam discovered that the placer mining could produce as much as fifty dollars a day. He also learned that the Griffith brothers, George F., John S., and David T. Griffith, fellow Kentuckians, had discovered good ore a mile west of Payne's Bar.[5] Although there is no evidence that the Griffiths and Womacks knew each other, it must have been encouraging to know that fellow Kentuckians had made good in the West.

Bolstered by such good news, Sam and Bob returned to Jackson County, Kentucky. Filled with enthusiasm, Sam told Corella and the children of the great opportunities in the Colorado Rocky Mountains. Within weeks Sam had found a buyer for the family farm. Corella and her daughters packed what family possessions were necessary, while Sam and his sons tended to sale of the livestock. Bob, who never cared for the farming or ranch life, was eager to return to the Colorado gold fields.

The trip west was planned for mid-summer, following a family wedding. The Womack's oldest daughter, sixteen year old Margaret, married Theodore Lowe, a Union officer. It was hoped that the couple would join the Womacks after the war.

Finally, in the summer of 1861, the Womack family left Kentucky, bound for a new life and the hope for riches in the high Colorado Rockies. The family first settled at Payne's Bar. Here, Sam became involved in several placer mining projects. With sons Bob and William, Sam began staking claims. Within a few years, Sam and his sons had discovered a rich silver vein in the rocky hills above the Griffith's new mining camp of Georgetown, so named for George T. Griffith. Here, father and sons established a stamp mill on Clear Creek.

Sam was so pleased with the potential for financial success that he wrote to his daughter Margaret and son-in-law, Theodore Lowe. Following the war, Colonel Theodore Lowe and his wife returned to their home state of Kentucky, where Lowe studied engineering at the local schools. The Lowe's readily accepted the invitation to come west.

In the summer of 1867, Margaret and Theodore Lowe, along with his brother, Emery, arrived in the growing mining town of Idaho Springs. Here, the Lowe brothers opened a business offering mining advice and assaying services to the prospectors in the area.

In late 1867, Sam sold his claim for ten thousand dollars to Lee R. Seaton.[6] Seaton would turn this claim into a profitable mine, producing a half million dollars annually for several years. The missed opportunity at fortune would later be repeated by his eldest son, Bob.

Nevertheless, Sam was quite pleased with the sale. With more money then ever before, Sam felt it was time to buy a farm or a ranch, which he considered a more suitable life for his wife and children. Sam and Corella set about looking for a place to settle. Nothing along the front range suited them. The couple traveled south to the Pikes Peak region where they stayed at Colorado City, a bustling pioneer town which briefly served as the Territorial Capital. While there, they made inquiries regarding available land in the area and were told of such prospects a few miles south of town on Fountain Creek. The couple made the journey to the Fountain Creek area. Sam and Corella liked the location and purchased land along Fountain Creek, approximately ten miles south of Colorado City.

Bob, now at the age of twenty-three, was not happy. The last thing he wanted to do was work on a ranch. During his time mining for gold and silver in the high Rocky Mountains, the unexplainable gold fever had crept into Bob, just as it had with thousands of prospectors who had followed the gold migration west for the taste of adventure and fortune. However, the dutiful son helped his father work the ranch that Sam had named the "Sunview Ranch," at least for a time.

While Bob deplored working on the ranch, he did enjoy riding the range on his favorite horse, a solid white steed he named Whistler. There are several legendary tales of Bob's expert horsemanship. For example, it is said he could lean down from his saddle and grab an object with his teeth. He could expertly guide Whistler in the thick of darkness, no matter where he was, or the obstacles, safely back to the family ranch.

From time to time, Bob would simply disregard his ranching duties altogether and ride into Colorado City where he would enjoy a few drinks at the bar with friends, Often, after several drinks, Bob would demonstrate his horsemanship by riding, at a full gallop, down the streets of Colorado City and shooting out the street lamps. Another legend has it that during one his many trips to the saloon in Colorado City, he actually rode Whistler into the saloon and up the stairs, a popular stunt for the era. Obviously, Bob's expert horsemanship demonstrations, while under the influence of alcohol, did not sit well with Sam. Therefore, Sam left the financial duties of the ranch to his younger daughter, twenty year old Eliza, who would prove to be a real asset for the family finances. From then on, she was known in the area as "Miss Lida." In the summer of 1870 Eliza Womack learned that Civil War hero, General William Jackson Palmer, was scouting a route along Fountain Creek for a rail line.[7] With a railroad came progress, something Eliza was fully aware of.

Eliza, and her brothers, Bob and William, each applied for a preemption land patent. (By this time, Margaret Booker Womack Lowe and her husband, Theodore, were living in Denver.) The land patents followed the same regulations as the Homestead Act of 1861, including the standard one hundred sixty acre allotment of land. However, the difference between the two government sponsored land deals was that the land patents, by 1870, were at the cost of $1.25 per acre up front. Eliza and her brothers paid the required sum. Sam Womack, as an established landowner, received the same land allotment free. Eliza had selected the four land patents very carefully, with each parcel situated along Fountain Creek. This gave the Womacks control of water rights for a land mass of just over six miles square. In time, the Womack's would have a herd of one thousand purebred Shorthorn cattle.

Meanwhile, about the same time that Eliza was securing additional land and water rights, General Palmer was busy acquiring his own parcels of land, some ten thousand acres, at the same price of $1.25 per acre, at the junction of Fountain and Monument Creeks, three miles east of the Womack's Sunview Ranch. It was near this area that Palmer formed the Fountain Colony, which would become Palmer's townsite of Colorado Springs. On October 21, 1871, Palmer's train steamed into the infant city.[8] The astute Eliza Womack must have been delighted with the future financial prospects the family land might mean to the progress of the new town. The next year, following the arrival of Palmer's Denver & Rio Grande railroad, the population of the area grew in exorbitant proportions. The Levi Welty family, close friends with the Womacks, were not pleased with the sudden intrusion of so many people. Levi Welty, a widower, had brought his daughter, Anna, and three sons, Alonzo, Frank and George, west from Ohio, arriving in the area in 1866. Welty received a homestead claim and water rights not far from where the Sam Womack family would later settle. However, with the development of Palmer's new town, various members of the town board began fighting Welty for his water rights. This is something Eliza Womack had considered when she strategically selected the four land patents for her family's ranch, with each parcel located on Fountain Creek. To Eliza's way of thinking, the growing town would pay handsomely for the water rights. Obviously, the town fathers had other ideas.

In the summer of 1872, Welty and his sons began looking for an alternative parcel of ranching land. Welty and the boys traveled over the historic Ute Pass to the picturesque Florissant Valley. The area was so named by Judge James Castello, who had settled in the area in 1870. Castello's small homestead was located at the junctions of East and West Twin Creeks. The good judge also ran a trading post where his best customers were the Ute Indians. [9]

It was at this trading post that the Weltys met Judge Castello. After inquiring about land prospects, Judge Castello told of great grazing land, suitable for a cattle ranch, just eighteen miles south of the area. The Weltys, father and sons, followed the judge's advice, making another trip over a mountain pass to the luscious green valley on the south side of Pikes Peak. Judge Castello's recommendation proved to be correct in all aspects. Before the end of the year 1872, Levi Welty sold his ranch, just north of the growing town of Colorado Springs, and acquired a homestead claim on the south side of Pikes Peak, at the eastern base of Mount Pisgah.

Welty and his sons brought their cattle operation to the valley in the south side shadow of Pikes Peak. There, Welty built a log cabin for his family and corrals, not far from the creek that flowed through his land, and set about raising cattle in the pristine valley. In an effort to keep the wildlife out of the creek near the corrals, Welty built an enclosure over the stream. In the process, a set of unforeseen circumstances resulted in naming the creek. As one of Welty's sons wrestled with a heavy log, he slipped and the log fell against him. Startled by the sudden injury to his son as Levi Welty ran to assist his son, his shotgun went off, which grazed his hand. The loud blast caused a skittish cow to bolt and break her leg when she fell into the creek. After a few moments as the commotion subsided and it was determined the Welty boy's injury was not serious, Levi Welty is said to have exclaimed: "Well boys, this is sure some cripple creek!" [10]

As with many family legends, stories tend to change over time. Years later, Mrs. Anna A. Welty Faulkner, the daughter of Levi Welty, recalled the naming of Cripple Creek during an interview with Dr. Francis W. Cragin of the Pioneer Museum in Colorado Springs:

> "A house was built on the Cripple Creek site in May of 1873. Levi, George, Frank and Alonzo put paper on the roof of the house. While they were at it, a valued calf stepped into a prairie dog hole and broke its leg. Then, Alonzo, while chopping wood, cut his foot so badly he was laid up for months. Someone said, 'We ought to call this Cripple Creek.'"

The legend of naming the little creek took a turn, so to speak, when Horace D. Bennett, who would later make a fortune in the area, recalled the event in a 1936 interview with the staff of the Pioneer Museum in Colorado Springs. Bennett stated:

> "An old cow had become mired in a bog along the stream's edge and, in extracting her, the cowboys had pulled so strong that one of the animal's legs became crippled. For several years she hobbled over the range and the cowboys had called the stream 'Cripple Creek' because of this accident."

Regardless of the true origin, the name stuck. From then on, the lush green meadows against sloping hills at the southwest base of Pikes Peak was known as the Cripple Creek area.

Bob Womack knew the area well. During his many wanderings away from the Sunview Ranch, Bob often rode through the valley hunting for wild game. At times he would also stop by the Welty place. In the fall of 1873, after Bob had informed his family how well Levi Welty was doing with his ranch, Sam sent telegrams to both his son-in-law Theodore Lowe and his brother, Emery Lowe. Sam was in need of their surveying abilities, as he intended to send his eldest son, Bob, to the Cripple Creek area to investigate the ranching possibilities.

It just so happened that the Lowe brothers had recently contracted with Dr. Ferdinand Vandeveer Hayden during a government sponsored survey of the West, including Colorado Territory. Dr. Hayden had been hired by the federal government in 1867 as "Geologist in Charge" to survey the geography of the western lands of the United States in an effort to open the area for permanent settlement. From 1873 to 1876, when Colorado would finally achieve statehood, the Hayden Survey team focused on the Rocky Mountain region.

Bob rode over Ute Pass to meet with the Lowe brothers who were already in the Cripple Creek area with Hayden and his crew of surveyors. Apparently the surveying team were impressed with their initial geological findings as Hayden's annual report to the government described the area as a "volcanic formation composed of trachyte and sylvanite."

Encouraged by the Hayden Survey's findings, Bob was eager to accept the invitation to lead another Hayden party into the area in the spring of 1874. During his short time with the survey crew, Bob witnessed more geological findings of promising mineral ore.

On August 1, 1876, Colorado became the thirty-sixth state to enter the union of the United States. That same summer, William Womack had returned from an extended trip to Kentucky with a bride. She was the former Ida Van Dyck.[12] Unfortunately, it was not long after the newlyweds had settled in at Sunview Ranch that it became obvious that Eliza did not get along with her new sister-in-law.

Both Sam and Eliza told William of the Hayden land survey in the Cripple Creek area and that the government was offering homestead claims. Sam suggested that William and Ida look over the land prospects and possibly apply for a homestead claim. Bob offered to take his brother over the pass and personally show him around the valley. William agreed.

As was his usual custom, Bob first stopped at the Welty place. Bob was stunned when Levi Welty informed him that because the valley would soon be opened up for more settlement, he was planning to sell his ranch. Welty and each of his sons had already filed for homesteads on the west side of Mount Pisgah at an area commonly known as the Four Mile Valley. After Bob explained why he and his brother were in the area, Welty readily offered his ranch to the Womack brothers for five hundred dollars.[13]

Bob and William wasted no time. They immediately returned home and presented Welty's offer to their father. After much discussion, it was agreed that William and Ida would purchase the Welty ranch. Bob decided he, too, would move to the Cripple Creek area.

Ever since Bob had witnessed the discoveries of promising mineral ore during his brief time with the Hayden Survey team the previous year, he had become increasingly curious as to the concept of rich ore in the area. Once again, the unexplainable gold fever had crept into Bob Womack.

While his brother and his wife were moving into the Welty cabin, Bob rode Whistler around the valley, looking for a suitable place of his own. He found it approximately two miles south of his brother's new ranch, at Arequa Gulch. Here, Bob built corrals for the cattle he later brought over from the Sunview Ranch. He stayed at William and Ida's new home, traveling back and forth daily.

After a few years of this routine, apparently Ida Womack's disposition became uncomfortable for Bob, so much so, that he found another place to live. Why Bob did not simply build a place to live at Arequa Gulch is unknown. What is known is that Bob acquired squatter rights to a parcel of land over a mile southeast of his brother's ranch. It was here, at an elevation of 9,600 feet, that Bob built a little cabin of his own, at the top of a ridge, in a place he named Poverty Gulch.[14]

From his cabin at Poverty Gulch, Bob rode Whistler southwest every day, following Cripple Creek, to care for the cattle at Arequa Gulch. Often along the way, Bob would examine the ground with a keen eye. It was a trait he had developed during his time in the mining towns of Idaho Springs and Georgetown.

Despite his limited education, Bob had learned quite a bit about mineral ores and geology. Therefore, Bob had become increasingly intrigued by Dr. F. V. Hayden's theory that the Cripple Creek area was the result of a "volcanic formation." Bob knew that if this theory was correct, many of the rocks would contain mineral ore, as would the gravel and sandstone in the creek bed. To Bob's way of thinking, it only stood to reason that a volcanic eruption eons ago would distribute the mineral ore in various forms all across the valley.

Bob Womack was correct in trusting Dr. F. V. Hayden's theory, as it was later confirmed by several geologists. An example is that of Geologist and Adjunct Professor at Emporia College, Steven Wade Veatch, who later wrote:

> "The Cripple Creek Mining District is centered on a small, circular-shaped, 32.7– million-year-old Oligocene volcanic complex that covers just over 18 square kilometers (seven square miles.) Gold is primarily present as gold-bearing telluride minerals in the district and is found in veins and surrounding rocks associated with the volcanic complex." [15]

Continuing with his working theory, Bob would explore the ground and the creek bed during his daily commute from his cabin at Poverty Gulch to the homestead at Arequa Gulch. For the next six years Bob stuck to his routine, always on the lookout for promising ore. On a spring day in May 1878, Bob stopped to visit his brother William at the old Welty place. During the visit, Bob allowed his horse, Whistler, to drink from the old Welty spring. After the visit, Bob went to the spring where he had tethered Whistler. As he was mounting his beloved horse, Bob spotted a large piece of gold-bearing float in the spring waters.

This was the first proof of Bob's theory, supported by the Hayden Survey claim, that the precious ore did indeed exist in the Cripple Creek area. Bob sent the float specimen to his brother-in-law, Theodore Lowe, in Denver, with the instruction to have it assayed. Receiving the ore specimen, Lowe complied with Womack's request. After taking the sample to several assayers, and gathering different opinions, in 1879, Lowe finally found an assayer who placed the value of the float at approximately two hundred dollars to the ton.

Receiving the assay report, Lowe made the trip to Cripple Creek to personally tell Bob the good news. It proved to be a serendipitous trip. While Lowe was in the Cripple Creek area, Eliza sent a telegram to Bob notifying him of the death of his mother, Corella Booker Womack. Eliza had also notified her sister, Margaret, in Denver, who joined the family at Colorado City. Bob, along with his brother William and his wife Ida, their two children, and Theodore Lowe, made the trip to Sunview Ranch for the funeral. Corella Booker Womack was the first to be buried in the Womack family plot in Colorado Spring's Evergreen Cemetery.[16]

Not long after the death of his mother, Bob and his brother-in-law, Theodore Lowe, set about working along Cripple Creek, much as they had with Clear Creek in the hills above Payne's Bar back in 1866. However, due to the "volcanic formation," of the Cripple Creek area, discovering the elusive high-grade ore proved to be very different than the two men had experienced at Payne's Bar, (later Idaho Springs) and Georgetown. Nevertheless, for the next three years Bob and Lowe persevered in the effort to discover the elusive ores they believed to have been released in the area of the "volcanic formation." However, the high green meadows against sloping hills in the valley, while providing good land for raising cattle, did not seem to hold much promise for ore riches. After three years, Lowe gave up on the idea and went back to Denver.

Although disappointed, Bob refused to give up. He still believed in his theory and was determined to prove it. Bob continued to explore just about every inch of ground on both sides of Cripple Creek as he followed it for nearly two miles to the point at the old Welty homestead, where he had originally found the ore-bearing float. It was a slow, steady process, but Bob had a purpose, to his way of thinking.

All the while, Bob continued to care for Womack's cattle herd in the valley, although not to the satisfaction of his sister, Eliza. A few times each year, Bob drove a selected number of cattle over Ute Pass and delivered them to the family's Sunview Ranch near Colorado City. After receiving his pay from his reluctant sister, Bob would often stop at the local saloon for a few drinks with old friends before returning to the valley of Cripple Creek. Plied with enough alcohol, Bob would talk about his gold theory, and everybody would laugh. "Crazy Bob," they called him, but almost everybody liked him.

One man that did believe in Womack's theory, was Henry Cocking, a Cornish miner who had made his way to the area from the rich mining area of Gilpin County, known as the "richest square mile on earth." Eventually, Cocking actually found promising ore and in 1881, he staked a claim not far from Womack's cabin in the hills above Poverty Gulch. After sinking a shaft and spending countless amounts of money, the claim was deemed worthless and Cocking left the area. Nevertheless, Cocking's mining activity brought a host of prospectors to the Cripple Creek region. Not all were honest. One of those men was William H.

"Chicken Bill" Lovell. Just the previous year, 1878, at Leadville, Lovell had stolen high-grade ore from Horace A. W. Tabor's legendary Little Pittsburgh mine on Fryer Hill and dropped it down the shaft of his mine on Carbonate Hill. [17] Lovell's act was known as "salting" a mine, a means to dupe prospective buyers. Arriving in the Cripple Creek area, he would soon repeat the scheme.

Lovell, along with an unknown accomplice, arrived in the region in the spring of 1884. They stopped at the homestead of Captain H. B. Grose, on Four Mile Creek, on the west side of Mount Pisgah. Grose, a Civil War veteran, operated an assaying service at his ranch, as well as a mine at Alma, Colorado. Not long after visiting with Captain Grose, the two men traveled approximately two miles, to the base of Mount McIntyre, where under the cloak of darkness, the men began digging a deep hole. When they were finished they placed a post with a wooden sign in the dirt pile next to the hole. The sign read: "Teller Placer, Twenty Acres S. J. Bradley, Locator Discovered April 5, 1884. Surveyed By D. G. Miller, M. E. April 7, 1884." [18]

A few days later, Captain Grose came upon the site. After reading the sign, Grose rode around the area but found no one present. Captain Grose left the area to alert friends and neighbors of the ore strike at Mount McIntyre in the Four Mile Valley. Within twenty-four hours, nearly three thousand prospectors converged on the site. [19]

Meanwhile, Lovell, along with his accomplice, had made their way to Salida, where they actually had their ore "sample" assayed. With the assayer results, two thousand dollars to the ton of ore, the men took the report to the press. Newspapers from Salida to Denver covered the story of the "new gold strike." However, somehow the location of the gold strike was referred to as Mount Pisgah, rather that Mount McIntyre.

Bob Womack was visiting with Frank Welty and his family at their ranch in the Four Mile Valley, when Captain Grose rode in with the news of a gold strike at Mount McIntyre. Bob was skeptical. He had ridden just about every area between mounts Pisgah and McIntyre, driving cattle and searching the ground for promising ore. Even so, Bob mounted Whistler and rode over to the area. He must have been astounded by what he saw. From the base of Mount McIntyre, for nearly a three-mile radius, thousands of prospectors swarmed the valley. It was a makeshift tent city complete with a saloon. Bob spent a few days in the area, examining the ground with his keen eye. At one point, undetected, Bob was able to grab a handful of the dirt at the discovery site. It was nothing but a heavy, wet, sticky mud substance. With Bob's mining experience, limited though it may have been, he knew this was not ore-bearing ground. Bob strongly suspected that this was another "hoax" that he had read about in the newspapers.

The term "hoax" with regard to prospectors and mining, was first used by the *Jefferson Inquirer*, in an editorial printed in the July 20, 1859, issue:

> "We have been somewhat amused in noticing the inscriptions, hoaxes and devices on the wagon covers of the Pike's [sic] Peak emigrants. One went through a day or two since, with a large elephant painted over the whole cover. Another had a rude attempt at a pike, with a pyramid to represent the Peak. But the most unequivocal inscription yet, we noticed on the wagon cover of a returned emigrant on Saturday. It read: 'Oh Yes! Pike's Peak in H---l and D---nation!'"

Bob was livid that such a hoax could be perpetuated in the Cripple Creek area. He immediately left the area and rode home to his cabin at Poverty Gulch. After his next cattle drive to Sunview Ranch, Bob followed his usual routine by stopping in Colorado City for a few drinks. Everyone was talking of the new gold strike. Because the newspaper reports had fixed the location of the gold strike at Mount Pisgah, Bob's friends at the bar bought him several rounds of drinks. When Bob tried to explain that that not only was the supposed gold discovery a hoax, but that the site was not at Mount Pisgah, but at Mount McIntyre his friends didn't care. "Crazy Bob," they called him, and ordered another round of drinks. While Bob enjoyed the free drinks, he left the saloon quite frustrated.

On his return trip home, Bob met two prospectors with several ore specimens from the Mount McIntyre area. After some discussion, Bob offered to take the ore samples to Colorado Springs to be assayed. Incredibly, the two prospectors agreed and left the specimens with Bob.

A few days later Bob rode over the pass to Colorado Springs, where he made a visit to an old friend at Colorado College. Dr. Henry Lamb, a metallurgist professor, and Bob often discussed the Hayden Survey and the theory of the "volcanic formation." Lamb believed in the theory, as did Bob. Bob respected Dr. Lamb and trusted him to do an honest assay of the ore specimens the two prospectors had entrusted him with. Lamb, who had been following the news of the gold strike, like everyone else, was only too happy to assay Bob's samples. When he had finished, he provided Bob with an assay report. Lamb must have been disappointed by what he did not find, as a portion of the report clearly shows no evidence of any precious metals:

> "Specimen No. Three, from claim twenty-five feet south of Teller Shaft. Gold, none; Silver, none. Specimen No. Seven, C. C. Rickard's claim, one quarter mile south from Teller Shaft. Gold, none; Silver, three-tenths of an ounce. Specimen No. Two, one and a half miles from Teller Shaft. Gold, one-tenth of an ounce." [20]

As disappointed as Lamb may have been, Bob was elated by the report. Finally he had proof that the supposed gold strike was a hoax, just as he knew it was all along. Armed with the report and the worthless specimens,

Bob attended a Colorado Springs town meeting. Here, he was introduced to one of the town board members, a merchant by the name of Marcellin L. DeCoursey. During the meeting that followed, DeCoursey repeatedly hailed the "Mount Pisgah" gold diggings, claiming it was good business for the merchants.

After the town meeting, Bob learned that DeCoursey had served under General William Jackson Palmer during the Civil War, rising to the rank of Captain. When General Palmer made plans for his new town, he encouraged DeCoursey to come west and be a part of it. Not long after the brief meeting between Bob and Captain DeCoursey, DeCoursey disclosed that he had learned, following the town meeting, that the "Mount Pisgah" gold diggings were indeed a hoax. It is not known if it was Bob Womack who alerted DeCoursey to the facts, although he had the evidence and the assay report when he met with the man. In any case, during the next town council meeting, Captain DeCoursey admitted his error, relating what he had apparently witnessed:

> "For a time this mine salter, Bradley, was able to keep the curious away from his bonanza but suspicion of him became so widespread that he pulled out of camp. Next day a large group of men dug a hole a few feet from Teller Placer. At the proper depth, a placer miner went down to investigate. General silence prevailed among the men packed around the top of the hole. Then the miner's head appeared. He glanced once around the crowd and said, 'We should-a hung the bastard.' " [21]

If Captain DeCoursey actually witnessed such an episode, it was obviously after he learned of the hoax, as just days before he had cried the virtues of what the gold findings meant for the business opportunities for Colorado Springs. Another curious point is that if this in fact took place, why wasn't the investigation of the Teller Placer conducted earlier, when in DeCoursey's own words, Bradley's actions had aroused concerns, stating "suspicion of him became so widespread that he pulled out of camp."

The *Colorado Springs Weekly Gazette* ran several editorials expressing their outrage at the obvious dubious actions of DeCoursey, a member of the town board. In one particular editorial, the editor opined:

> "5,000 on Mr. Bradley's invitation spent $30 each on transportation alone - $150,000.00. How much of that went to Canon City? The Denver papers boomed Mount Pisgah for the D. & R. G. Railroad. Thousands followed their advice and paid $6.40 each way to Canon City and back. Canon City stage men took them to the mines for $5.00. Colorado Springs could have got them there for half as much." [22]

The D. & R. G. Railroad mentioned in the *Weekly Gazette* editorial, was General William Jackson Palmer's Denver & Rio Grande Railroad. While the editorial was correct in questioning the actions of Bradley and his hoax, it was a bold statement by the editor to call out the operators of the railroad owned by Palmer, the Colorado Springs town founder.

Shortly after the episode of the "Mount Pisgah" hoax, the health of Bob's father, Samuel Redd Womack, began to fail. It was also during this time that the family learned that Ida, William Womack's wife, was pregnant with her third child. William and Ida announced to the family that they had made the decision to move back to their native state of Kentucky.

With this news, the Womack family made plans to not only sell the William Womack homestead, the former Welty ranch, but also sell Bob's place at Poverty Gulch, as well as the Sunview ranch near Colorado City. Eliza enlisted the assistance of her brother-in-law, Theodore Lowe, to sell the properties. Within a few months Lowe had found a buyer for both homesteads and the William Womack family moved back to Kentucky. However, a buyer for the Sunview Ranch never emerged. The buyer for the Womack land was a Denver merchant, Fred Thompson, who owned a furniture store on Lawrence Street. Thompson soon went into partnership with another Denver businessman, Frank Anderson, who had recently purchased a homestead not far from the old Welty place. With the properties between the two men, Thompson and Anderson formed the "Pikes Peak Land and Cattle Company." Not only did they have over six hundred acres, but they also held control of the water rights.

Not long after the two men announced the formation of the new company, Bob Womack rode Whistler over to the office of the new land company and introduced himself to Thompson and Anderson. After some considerable discussion the three men came to a mutual business proposition. It was agreed that Bob would continue to live in his cabin above Poverty Gulch in exchange for riding the range, caring for the cattle, and doing various other jobs as the need arose.

It was not long before Bob realized how much he enjoyed cowpunching for his new employers. As the land company's holdings stretched from eastern base of Mount Pisgah west to include a sizable portion of the Four Mile area, Bob could ride Whistler from one end of company's land to the other, and be gone for days. One summer he spent an entire week at George Welty's ranch and even attended a dance where Welty played the fiddle. What Bob really appreciated was that his employers did not pester him as his sister Eliza had. Bob Womack finally had the freedom he had craved for so long.

In July 1885, two strangers rode up to Bob's cabin. They introduced themselves as real estate partners Horace D. Bennett and Julius Myers. During a long conversation, Bob learned that the two men were interested in purchasing the Pikes Peak Land and Cattle Company, and asked Bob if he would show them around the property holdings. Bob agreed and for the next few days, Bob did just that. During the excursion,

Bennett often remarked on the lush green meadows of the valley against the sloping hills, but grumbled about the dilapidated condition of the various buildings, particularly the William Womack cabin, (the old Welty cabin) which served as the headquarters for the Pikes Peak Land and Cattle Company. Conversely, Myers extolled the virtues of the scenic area, the rich grazing land and the opportunity to eventually break up the land for smaller ranch sales. Evidently, Horace D. Bennett did not have a high opinion of Bob Womack. In a 1936 interview with the staff of the Pioneer Museum in Colorado Springs. Bennett remarked:

> "We called him 'Crazy Bob.' He was employed when we acquired the land but found him to be an indifferent cowboy. He liked to ride a horse about the country at a run until the animal was exhausted."

There is no known or written history as to how or why Bennett's dislike of Womack came about. However, by his statement, the disdain is clear. Bob Womack was an avid horseman. He tended to every horse on every ranch he ever worked on with the same care he provided for his favorite horse, Whistler. The very idea of riding "until the animal was exhausted," was something no horseman, including Bob would ever do. More over, when Bob roamed the range, in nearly every excursion, he did so at a slow pace, in an effort to keep one eye on the cattle and the other on the ground looking for promising ore.

Nevertheless, after much discussion between Myers and Bennett, who also crunched the numbers with pad and pencil, the real estate partners agreed to purchase the land as well as the buildings from the Pikes Peak Land and Cattle Company. As Denver-based realtors, with an office on Larimer Street, Bennett and Myers had no intention of personally overseeing their new land acquisition. With heavy advertisement in the *Rocky Mountain News*, the real estate firm of Bennett and Myers was able to secure the services of a Kansas cattleman, George Carr, to run their Cripple Creek operation.

In the fall of 1885, George and Emma Carr, along with their children and Emma's brother, Jack Edwards, arrived in the Cripple Creek area. Curiously, one of the first things George Carr did upon his arrival was change the name of the former Pikes Peak Land and Cattle Company to the "Broken Box Ranch," perhaps a reference to the many dilapidated buildings found in various locations over the six hundred acres of ranching property.

Being hospitable, as well as looking to continue his employment, Bob rode over to meet the Carr family. Bob and George immediately hit it off and formed a long-lasting friendship. Carr even bucked the authority of his employers when he hired Bob to look after the cattle interests.

Carr trusted Bob to ride the range and care for the cattle. Bob respected Carr and worked hard for his friend and employer, all the while keeping his keen eye on the ground and creeks as he rode the range. On a crisp fall day in 1886, Bob staked a claim on the northern slope above Poverty Gulch. Because of the splendid mountain scenery at the spot, nearly two thousand feet above his cabin, Bob named his claim the "Grand View." Bob took a few samples to his trusted friend, Dr. Henry Lamb in Colorado Springs. Lamb's assay revealed such a high trace of gold content, that on October 13, 1886, Bob legally recorded the claim. During that winter Bob spent his free time working his claim as the weather permitted.

That same spring, Edwin Wallace arrived from Colorado Springs and offered Bob five hundred dollars for a two-thirds interest in the Grand View claim. Bob readily agreed to the partnership. On April 23, 1887, Wallace returned with a wagonload of mining equipment and a bank draft for Bob. Throughout the summer, the two partners worked the claim and filed a few more claims as well. For the next year, Wallace and Womack worked their claims with little success. Then in the spring of 1889, Bob received another visitor, an old friend, Dr. Grannis, at his cabin at Poverty Gulch.

Doctor John P. Grannis, a native of Ohio, had come to Colorado Springs in 1886 to relieve his tubercular condition, as did thousands of people with respiratory ailments. With his improved health, Grannis established a successful dental practice, with the Womack family counted among his many patients.

Over the years, Bob and Dr. Grannis often discussed the possibility of gold in the Cripple Creek area. Bob told Grannis of the "volcanic" theory of gold buried deep in the crust of the earth at Cripple Creek. Bob also told Grannis of his own theory, developed long before he had discovered the gold-bearing float at his brother's homestead in 1878. Bob's theory was that the gold-bearing float had obviously washed down into the creeks and rivers over thousands of years. Intrigued, Grannis would occasionally prospect with Bob.

This was the reason for Grannis' arrival in the spring of 1889. For the next few days, Bob showed the dentist around the area, pointing out the direction he believed the gold-bearing float likely came from, and took him to his various claims. Evidently, Grannis must have liked what he saw as he agreed to grubstake Bob. True to his word, on December, 2, 1889, Grannis returned to Bob's cabin with a bank draft for five hundred dollars.

Not only was Bob grateful for Grannis' monetary support, he was bolstered by Grannis' friendship and belief in him. During that winter, while Bob stuck to the same routine as the previous winter, working his claims when weather permitted, he did so with renewed energy.

During the early spring of 1890, Bob dug shafts and worked his Grand View claim in earnest. As the spring temperature warmed the earth, Bob watched with great interest as the small streams in the area, and particularly Cripple Creek, began to swell from the mountain runoff. Bob rode Whistler along the creeks and streams, studying the roaring waters with his keen eye. Bob was looking for that elusive high-grade gold-bearing float that had evaded him for the past twenty years, ever since the gold fever had crept into Bob, at Payne's Bar. Through due diligence, Bob did discover several pieces of what he thought might be good float. Unfortunately, Professor Lamb's assays proved otherwise. As spring rolled into summer, Bob had had very little to show for his efforts.

Bob spent the cool autumn months back at Poverty Gulch, where he put all of his energy into digging deeper shafts at his Grand View claim. It was hard work, but with his pick and shovel Bob was able to dig a four-foot shaft to a depth of approximately ten feet. When he completed this task, Bob loaded the dirt into buckets and hauled them away from the shaft. By October, Bob had managed to dig a second shaft in the same manner, and this shaft was even deeper than the first. One day, as Bob was climbing up the ladder from this shaft, with one hand hoisting a bucket of dirt, he happened to glance at the rock wall. There was a shining glimmer in the rock he had never seen before. After disposing of his bucket of dirt, Bob quickly climbed back down the ladder with pick in hand.

After a considerable time of picking at the rock surface, Bob was able to uncover a deep crevice in the rock. In the midst of this crack was a discolorization that Bob knew to be gold ore.

What Bob Womack did not know at the time, was that with this discovery of gold, he would effectively launch not only the last gold rush in America, his discovery in Cripple Creek would become known world-wide as the "Greatest Gold Camp on Earth."

Robert Miller "Bob" Womack about the time of his gold discovery. (Denver Public Library, Western History Department, F-22733)

General William Jackson Palmer was the founding father of Colorado Springs and played an important role in Eliza Womack's land and water rights. (Denver Public Library, Western History Department, Z-10)

Alonzo Welty, son of Levi Welty, was a friend to the Womack brothers. (Denver Public Library, Western History Department, Z-22598)

The Welty cabin was purchased by Bob and William Womack for $500. (Denver Public Library, Western History Department, X-11)

Businessmen at an early cabin in Bob Womack's Poverty Gulch. (Denver Public Library, Western History Department, X-707)

Few people lived in the area when Bob Womack filed his gold claim in 1890. (Denver Public Library, Western History Department, X-826)

Chapter 2

Colorado Cowpoke Discovers Gold

On that cool, crisp autumn day in 1890, there was no doubt in Bob Womack's mind that he had uncovered a rich vein of gold.

After spending a considerable time examining the half-inch discolorized vein in the rock surface, Bob decided to use dynamite in an effort to break loose the ore. Bob used his rock drill to bore a thirty-inch hole a few inches away from the vein. Then he carefully placed a single eight-inch stick of dynamite in the drilled hole. Bob placed a second dynamite stick fused with the first. After fusing yet a third stick of dynamite, Bob climbed up the ladder, unrolling a five-foot fuse as he made his ascent out of the shaft. Once outside the shaft, Bob stretched the fuse line as far as he could and struck a match. Then he ran for cover.

Within a minute of lighting the fuse, all of Poverty Gulch rocked from the explosion. For the next few days, Bob shoveled the pile of dirt that the blast had created. Then he again set about dynamiting near the surface of the vein. Finally, Bob was able to dislodge a portion of the ore held in the deep crack of the rock.

After retrieving as many ore samples as he could, Bob carefully laid out a rectangular area on the north peak above Poverty Gulch, some three hundred by fifteen hundred feet, next to the shaft, in an effort to expand his mining claim. Then he attached a handwritten sign to a wooden post and drove it into the ground. The sign read:

"El Paso Claim Located October 20, 1890 By R. M. Womack and Dr. John Grannis Mining District Unknown" [1]

The following day, Bob rode Whistler over the pass to tell Dr. Grannis of his find and to register the new claim. Bob then paid a visit to his friend, Professor Harry Lamb, who readily agreed to assay Bob's ore samples.

The metallurgist professor spent the next several days in the laboratory at Colorado College, carefully analyzing the specimens. When he was finished, Dr. Lamb wrote out his assay report. Two of Bob's ore samples had assayed as high as $250 to the ton. [2]

Bob Womack was quite pleased, but not surprised by the results of Dr. Lamb's assay. Nevertheless, it must have been an overwhelming sense of euphoria for forty-six year old Bob Womack, to have finally, after nearly two decades, located the gold vein he knew all along was there. It wasn't so much that he was looking to get rich, but to discover the elusive vein and piece together that incredible jigsaw puzzle of rock formations and erosion causing threads of high grade ore running rampant amidst the incredible volcanic formation of the Cripple Creek area.

Despite the fabulous assay report, Bob's immediate dilemma was lack of funds to develop the new El Paso gold claim and improve the original Grand View mine. For the next few weeks, Bob and his partner, Dr. John Grannis, met with a few mining experts in the Colorado Springs area, showing them the ore samples, as well as Dr. Lamb's assay report. Because of the unusual gray color of the specimens, which was not present in previous Colorado gold strikes, the mining men showed little, if any interest.

During a conversation with a trusted friend, Dr. Grannis expressed his frustration over the lack of interest in Womack's gold specimens. Dr. Grannis' friend, Harry Seldomridge, offered to display one of the ore samples in the front window of his father's store. Grannis agreed and gave him one of the gold-bearing specimens. For several weeks Womack's gold-bearing ore sat in the window of the J. F. Seldomridge & Sons grain store on Tejon Street in Colorado Springs.

Dr. Grannis also visited with Hiram Rogers, a reporter with the Weekly Gazette newspaper. After an extensive conversation, Rogers declined to write about Bob Womack's find. Sometime later, Rogers wrote with obvious indifference of his missed journalistic opportunity:

> "I remember seeing Bob's latest ore with indifferent curiosity, for who that has lived in the Rocky Mountains has not been shown oceans of such stuff that came from a future bonanza? As a newspaper man I looked Dr. Grannis up and asked him about it. His replies were not sufficient to impress me, and I let it pass. Naturally, a discovery by Bob Womack was discounted in Colorado Springs."

With no means to adequately develop his mining claims, Bob returned to Poverty Gulch to work the mines himself. Day after day Bob would take his hammer and chisel and slowly chip away at the ore vein. Collecting the pieces and chunks of the gray-colored ore, Bob would carefully place them in a grain sack and haul them down the mountain slope to his cabin. By the time the winter snows fell over the Cripple Creek area, Bob had plenty of ore, but no buyers.

While Bob spent the fall of 1890 working his claims, Dr. Grannis made a habit of stopping by the grain store of Seldomridge & Sons on a weekly basis. During one of his visits, Grannis noticed a gentleman inspecting Womack's ore specimens. Grannis introduced himself to the man, who was Ed De LaVergne. After a conversation centered around mining, of which De LaVergne professed great interest, Grannis suggested that De LaVergne take a few courses in metallurgy and assaying from Professor Harry Lamb at the Colorado College.

Grannis had known the De LaVergne family for years, but this was the first time he had met the youngest of the four children. The De LaVergne family hailed from Marietta, Ohio, where Edward Morton De LaVergne was born in 1846. With news of the impending civil war between the states, the elder De LaVergne moved his family westward. However, George, the eldest of the De LaVergne children, stayed behind and joined the war effort, serving with the Eighth Tennessee Mounted Regiment. By the end of the war, George De LaVergne had received the rank of Colonel. Following the war, Colonel George De LaVergne rejoined his family. The De LaVergne family arrived in Colorado Springs in 1878. Within a few years, the family opened a furniture store, directly across the street from the Seldomridge & Sons grain store on South Tejon Street. During this time, Ed De LaVergne, with his keen interest in mining, worked at several mining districts across the west, including southwestern Colorado and New Mexico. Unable to make a sustainable living, Ed De LaVergne had returned to his family in the fall of 1890.

De LaVergne took the advice of Dr. Grannis, and enrolled in Professor Henry Lamb's classes at Colorado College. To pay for the classes, De LaVergne worked part-time at the family's furniture store. There, he formed a friendship with the store's manager, Fred Frisbee, who shared De LaVergne's interest in mining.

When De LaVergne completed his courses at Colorado College, in December 1890, he received the formal certification as an assayer. A few days later, he remembered seeing Womack's ore samples displayed in the window of the Seldomridge & Sons grain store, across the street from his family's furniture store. One day, during a break at the family business, De LaVergne crossed the street to take another look at the ore specimens.

De LaVergne had learned of the Hayden Survey and the "volcanic formation" theory from Professor Lamb, and agreed with Professor Lamb's assay report of Womack's ore specimens. De LaVergne asked Lamb to arrange a meeting with Bob Womack. After a few days, Lamb set up the meeting at Colorado College. In attendance were De LaVergne, Lamb, Dr. Grannis, and Bob Womack.

During the meeting, Lamb explained in detail the volcanic theory established during the 1873 Hayden Survey and Bob's involvement with the survey team. Bob explained to De LaVergne that while he believed in the theory, he had also found several pieces of gold-bearing float in the creeks and streams of the Cripple Creek area over the dozen years he had lived there. De LaVergne developed an interest that the possibility of a real wealth of gold hidden at and near Womack's mining claims at Poverty Gulch existed. De LaVergne politely asked Bob's permission to visit his mining claims and explore the Cripple Creek area.

In mid-January 1891, Ed De LaVergne and Fred Frisbee left the De LaVergne furniture store for a prospecting trip at Poverty Gulch. After reaching the area, the two men called on George and Emma Carr at the Broken Box Ranch, where the couple graciously invited them to stay during their time in Cripple Creek. De LaVergne and Frisbee spent three weeks exploring the region. They found a few sites which they believed quite possibly contained promising ore. Before they returned to Colorado Springs with their ore samples, De LaVergne and Frisbee staked off two claims, both on the same slope above Poverty Gulch as Bob Womack's claims. De LaVergne and Frisbee's El Dorado Lode claim was located on the western edge of Womack's El Paso claim. Just below these claims, was the Mollie Kathleen mine, located on September 12, 1891, by Mrs. Mollie Kathleen, who became the first female miner in the region. [3]

Over the next few months, word got around throughout the Cripple Creek area that mining claims were being staked out across the region. Perhaps it was George and Emma Carr who spread the word, as they had hosted De LaVergne and Frisbee who ultimately filed the first mining claims since Bob Womack's El Paso claim in October 1890.

In any case, George Carr and a few friends, including Marion C. Lankford, J. S. Lentz, and William Spell, formed a group and filed a few claims of their own. William Spell's son, Leslie Doyle Spell, later recounted his recollection of his father's entry into prospecting:

> "Father discussed the plans he had made with Carr. The four men grubstaked and outfitted Lankford who was eager to start out immediately. However, he was persuaded to wait until the weather moderated, so in February of 1891, Lankford traveled up into one of the gulches about a mile and a half from the Carr ranch. There he discovered a gold-bearing vein. Upon his return to Florrisant with his ore samples, Handburry and Lintz recommended that dad return with Lankford and help with locations. Dad was only too willing, so he and Lankford proceeded to locate five claims, endeavoring to follow the trend of the vein. These claims were named the Robert E. Lee, the Blanche, the Hobo, the Panhandle, and the Blue Bell. There was no road east of the Carr ranch so the Blue Bell partners were forced to build a crude road to the claims. Mr. Carr, while doing assessment work on the Hobo claim in a gulch and near the top of one of the small mountains, later known as Guyot Hill, unearthed the grave of an Indian squaw. Thereafter this gulch was known as Squaw Gulch, which name it carries to this day." [4]

William Spell had first met Bob Womack at the Carr's Broken Box Ranch in the winter of 1889. Years later, Leslie Doyle Spell recalled the occasion:

> "At the Broken Box Ranch, as Carr's domain was known, we were warmly greeted by Mrs. Carr, our gracious hostess.

Several of the neighbors from from surrounding ranches were also gathered there for a roundup and branding. This roundup, incidentally, was to be the last one held at the Broken Box. One man I remember in particular - the old prospector, Bob Womack, who was spending the winter with the Carrs, doing chores, mending fences and helping with the cattle. As is customary with prospectors, young and old, all he could talk about was the wonderful finds he was going to make in his search for gold. Dad, always a good listener, became quite an interested subject for Womack to work upon and was almost convinced enough to grubstake him. After hearing Bob's story dad asked Mr. Carr if there was really anything to his glowing tale. Carr replied that frequently Womack would find samples that would assay fairly well and then again fail to find anything at all, but persisted in searching for the source of the float samples he would find. Several parties had become interested at times and grubstaked Bob. While Bob and my father were spending hours in front of the fireplace in the old Womack cabin where we were lodged during that memorable housewarming of 1890, and discussing Bob's wonderful prospects, I also was listening with intense interest. If I had been a grown man then I am sure Bob and I would have been partners in his gold venture, for all of my life I have carried the lure of prospecting in my veins." [5]

The news of the many mining claims near the Cripple Creek area quickly reached the Colorado Springs area. Hiram Rogers, the same reporter with the *Weekly Gazette* newspaper, who had previously declined to report on Bob Womack's incredible gold find, took the opportunity to, in typical journalistic fashion, to correct his error. In the February 22, 1891, issue of the paper, under the headline, "The Reported Gold!," Rogers wrote:

"The talk about the find brought to light a matter that the Gazette had promised to keep quiet until better developments gave it foundation. About one month ago a young ranchman well known in the city came here to report that he had found a vein of rich ore. A company has been formed with Dr. J. P. Grannis at its head. A claim has been staked and recorded. The find is eighteen miles south of Florissant and not far from Mount Pisgah."

Rogers' explanation is shallow at best. It was Dr. Grannis who brought the story of the "vein of rich ore" to Rogers, not the "young ranchman," whom, interestingly, Rogers does not name. It is also worth noting that Rogers placed Florissant first in his piece, ahead of Mount Pisgah, which was the vicinity of the referred "vein of rich ore" of Womack's find.

Nevertheless, Bob Womack was well aware of the gold diggings in the Florissant area. After all, George Carr and William Spell, two of the men who had located some of those claims, were his friends. Bob rode over to the Florissant area to explore the mining prospects. Bob was astounded to see the rapid development of the Blue Bell claim. William Spell had developed the area around his mine, and purchased a wagon particularly designed to haul heavy loads. As the ore was extracted from the mine, the hired wagon driver, Richard "Dick" Dickerson, hauled the wagonload of ore to the small town of Florissant. From there the ore was transported by train to the smelter at Colorado City. William Spell's son, Leslie Doyle Spell, later recounted:

"This was the first carload of ore shipped from what later became the Cripple Creek District. The Blue Bell ore contained about 30 percent lead and was the only ore containing lead ever found in the area. The highest assay ran $175 a ton in gold, silver and lead, but the ore shipped did not run that high. Smelter returns to the Blue Bell Mining Company amounted to $1,930.00 for the entire shipment of thirty tons. This momentous shipment was the only one shipped from the district in the year 1891." [6]

While Bob did some prospecting, he also spent a fair amount of time visiting with his friends including Carr, Spell, and Ed De LaVergne. After some discussion among Bob and his friends, it was agreed that the miners would hold an open meeting to establish a legitimate mining district, complete with rules and regulations.

On Sunday, April 5, 1891, the meeting was held at the Broken Box Ranch in the home of George and Emma Carr. Several local ranchers attended, including Captain H. B. Grose and wife, and Levi Welty and his sons. Over a dozen area miners were in attendance including Ed De LaVergne, Fred Frisbee, William Spell and his son, Leslie, Marion Lankford and Bob Womack. As everyone took their seats, De LaVergne addressed the group, asking for all to agree that with Bob Womack's gold discovery, the original Gold King, now the El Paso, Womack was indeed the first to discover gold in the Cripple Creek region. There was unanimous agreement. With that impromptu piece of businesses dispensed with, De LaVergne turned the meeting over to William Spell. Leslie Doyle Spell, later recounted the events of that momentous meeting:

"The foregoing procedure is what happened in the early part of 1891 of the Mount Pisgah gold excitement. My father, Bill Spell, was the man who encouraged holding the first meeting. Dad had received much of his information as to procedure from Bob McLain, the young man we had met the previous summer, and whom had been employed as foreman of the Blue Bell mine. It was dad who served as temporary chairman and opened the meeting. George Carr was the first elected chairman, but the name of the secretary has slipped my memory. A committee was formed to write [mining] camp rules and regulations."

George Carr created a second committee, headed by Ed De LaVergne, to stake out the boundaries of the new mining district. Carr then asked the group to offer suggestions for the name of the new mining district. Among the names bandied about were, "Mount Pisgah Mining District," "Cripple Creek Mining District," and "Womack Mining District." After the votes were cast by the attendees, "Cripple Creek Mining District" received the most votes, with "Womack Mining District" a close second. Thus, the Cripple Creek Mining District was duly formed.

After De LaVergne and his committee had studied the geography of the region, the committee wrote the mining laws of the new mining district which were presented and agreed to at the second group meeting. Again, the meeting was held at the Broken Box Ranch. Leslie Doyle Spell recounted the event:

"This historic meeting was held on a hillside of the Carr ranch around a bonfire. At this meeting, dad [William Spell] was appointed camp marshal since he already held a commission as deputy sheriff of El Paso County. Not only was dad saddled with the marshal's job but the recording of mining claims as well, as the elected recorder flunked on the job, with the books landing in dad's lap. Until the summer of 1893 those books, the main being a large leather-backed ledger, remained in our home. I can remember dad working over that ledger by lamplight in the evening and the care he bestowed on it, with strict orders to us children never to touch it, Those records were later transferred to the Blue Bell office on Bennett Avenue in Cripple Creek." [8]

De LaVergne explained to the group that, by using the 1878 Hayden Survey maps, and keeping in mind the "volcanic formation" theory, he and his committee had established the district boundaries as Rhyolite Mountain being the northern border, and Squaw Mountain as the southern border. The eastern border was designated by Bull Hill, and Mount Pisgah served as the western border. This area encompassed nearly seven square miles, just over twenty-three thousand acres.

During this meeting, the new district's mining laws were established. Following the United States Mining laws, established after the California gold rush of 1849. It was unanimously decided that each prospector could claim as much as ten acres per claim, provided said claim was legally filed with the El Paso county clerk in Colorado Springs. An unlimited group of prospectors could file claims on adjoining claims, not to exceed one hundred twenty acres. During that summer of 1891, the new Cripple Creek Mining District bustled with prospectors from all over the region and from as far away as Leadville, Aspen and Creede. Within a short amount of time, a group of miners had established a small mining camp. Soon, tents were erected from the base of Mount Pisgah, east to Womack's Poverty Gulch.

However, one man who did not take Womack's gold strike seriously was the former El Paso County Clerk, Irving Howbert, who later wrote of the those early days:

> "Early in the year 1891, there began to be much talk in Colorado Springs concerning the discovery of gold on the west side of Pike's [sic] Peak, but those who were familiar with mining had little faith in the reports. One reason for this was that a few years previously there had been much excitement over reported gold discoveries near Mount Pisgah, in that locality, which was quickly over since the reports proved to have little basis. Late in 1889, a mining engineer of experience told me that gold actually had been found by an old miner near the headwaters of Four Mile Creek on the west side of Pike's Peak, and advised me to

investigate the matter. But, knowing the miner to be an erratic sort of fellow, I gave the report little further attention, believing that if there had been anything of value in that region, it would have been found long before. Consequently, when rumors of gold discoveries in the same locality were repeated in 1891, I gave them slight notice." [9]

Howbert's seemingly disinterested account of the new mining activity in the Cripple Creek region is a bit naive, at best. After all, Howbert's brother, Frank, had succeeded him as county clerk for El Paso County. Therefore, it was Frank Howbert who recorded Womack's 1891 El Paso mining claim, as well as the subsequent claims of the Blue Bell, Blanche, Hobo, Panhandle and Robert E. Lee, in February 1891. Howbert could not have been more wrong. By the end of that first year of ore production, the Cripple Creek Mining District had extracted over two hundred thousand dollars worth of gold. [10]

Further evidence of Irving Howbert's underestimation of the Cripple Creek gold strike was the amount of coverage this new gold rush was receiving in newspapers all over the state. The February 28, 1891, issue of the *Rocky Mountain News* devoted the entire front page to the sensational story. Under the headline, "Cripple Creek," the page included a detailed map of the Cripple Creek Mining District, including names and locations of the various mines. In a separate article, under the headline, "The New Gold Camp Is Making Regular Shipments," the piece included the production amounts:

"The Lincoln mine has shown assays of $28 to $40 gold. The Great Vippew gave an average of $35. The Rose Maud produced "three selected sacks assayed at over $2,000. The Buena Vista shied one carload that gave a return of $142 per ton."

The "Great View" mentioned in the *Rocky Mountain News* article, was actually Bob Womack's "Grand View" mine. Womack had spent the past year developing both his Grand View and El Paso gold claims virtually on his own, save for another six hundred dollars grubstake from Dr. Grannis. Bob managed to sink another six-foot shaft in both the Grand View and El Paso claims. During hours of backbreaking work, Bob hauled gold-bearing ore to the surface. Leslie Doyle Spell, nine years old at the time, along with his brother, spent many summer days with Bob at his mining claims. Years later Spell wrote:

> "During the summer of 1891 Wendall Carr, brother Oakley and I played around in the prospect holes where Bob had discovered his rock which he maintained carried gold. His holes were dug along an alluvial wash, near solid rock. He moved his interests on up the gulch to where he located his Gold King group of mining claims. That claim, in my opinion was his original El Paso claim." [11]

By February 1891, when the *Rocky Mountain News* first reported the Cripple Creek gold strike, over five thousand people had swarmed to the area. The *Rocky Mountain News* continued to cover the events. In the April 29, 1891, issue, under the headline, "Cripple Creek," the paper reported:

> "Results Exceeding the Fair Promise of the February Showing. Two months is a brief period in the life of the ancient hills. But it is a period ample for mighty deeds when thousands, over eight thousand, of sturdy western men are sending the ring and clang of their picks along the mountain side."

With so much activity in the Cripple Creek Mining District, a group of prospectors decided to turn the little mining camp into a town. Streets were laid out on land that bordered the north and east sections of the Broken Box Ranch property which Horace Bennett and Julius Myers had purchased in 1885. The men called their new town "Hayden Placer," in honor of Doctor Ferdinand Vandeveer Hayden, who had surveyed the region in 1873. However, it would be some time before they would formally plat and record the town with the El Paso county clerk. Even so, the "unofficial" townsite of Hayden Placer had been granted an "official" post office from the government, named "Fremont." William "Bill" Gowdy served as postmaster, receiving a government salary of eighteen dollars a month.

The news of the proposed Hayden Placer townsite quickly reached the Denver real estate office of Horace Bennett and Julius Meyers. Alarmed by the proximity of this "townsite" to their property, the two realtors left Denver, bound for the Cripple Creek District.

Arriving in the Cripple Creek District, Bennett and Myers were amazed at what they saw. The area was slowly resembling a a growing frontier town. The tents that originally dominated the camp were steadily being replaced with small wooden homes. The lumber was supplied by a new sawmilling business started by Samuel Altman at the Womack's Poverty Gulch site. [12]

Seizing a golden opportunity, as it were, the city slicker duo of Bennett and Meyers decided to file a townsite plat on their Broken Box Ranch property. The realtors had eighty acres of their land surveyed and platted. On November 4, 1891, the firm of Bennett and Myers officially filed their new townsite plat.[13] They called it "Fremont," hoping to capitalize on the official government post office name.

The new town of Fremont consisted of five streets running from north to south, with each street numbered "First" through "Fifth," from the west to the east, ending at the edge of Poverty Gulch. Four streets ran from east to west. The main street of commerce was laid out on a small hill where the south side of the street was well over twelve feet lower than the north side at one point. This street was named Bennett Avenue after Horace Bennett. The street in the business section south of Bennett Avenue was named Myers Avenue after Julius Myers. The other two streets were named after George Carr and former Colorado governor, Benjamin H. Eaton. [14]

Bennett and Myers sold the business lots for fifty dollars and the other lots at twenty-five dollars. Bennett took one of the lots at the northeast corner of Second Street and built one of the first hotels, the Windsor. Soon Bennett Avenue boasted several businesses, including a bank, a mining stock broker, as well as a number of saloons. With this economic boom, Samuel Altman's sawmill business was perhaps the most profitable in the growing town.

The success thus far of Bennett and Myers' town of Fremont did not go unnoticed by the founders of the fledging bordering mining town of Hayden Placer. At the urging of Edward M. De LaVergne, the founders of the Hayden Placer townsite officially filed for the platted townsite with the El Paso county clerk. However, for some unknown reason, approval of the townsite plat was received many months later, on February 15, 1892. Meanwhile, William Spell, one of the first mine owners, who also served as an El Paso County sheriff deputy, agreed to provide security for Hayden Placer.[15] Within weeks, the mining camp was bustling with new activity, businesses were established and tents were slowly replaced with wooden structures, with lumber supplied from Altman's sawmill. As Hayden Placer began to thrive with new businesses, a rivalry grew between the two mining towns.

Meanwhile, a friend of Ed De LaVergne, Count James M. Pourtales, an emigrant from Germany, made an exploratory trip to the Cripple Creek District at the behest of De LaVergne. Count Pourtales, a member of the Huguenot family, arrived in Colorado in 1884, where upon with his enormous wealth, the Count, immediately set about making various business investments. One of the investments a worthless dairy farm in 1885, at the base of Cheyenne Mountain in Colorado Springs. This land would eventually be developed for the Broadmoor Hotel. Within five years, Pourtales had purchased much of the surrounding land. Pourtales then built a large community building and formed the Cheyenne Mountain Country Club, which opened on July 4, 1891. It was at this new establishment that De LaVergne and Pourtales met to discuss the mining prospects at the Cripple Creek Mining District. A month after the meeting, Count Pourtales and a friend, Thomas C. Parrish, who had experience at mining, arrived in the mining district. For days, the two men rode from one end of the district to the other, talking with the miners and studying the region. As Ed De LaVergne was busy enticing Pourtales to invest in the district's mining prospects, Bob Womack was doing the same. During that summer, Bob rode Whistler over the pass to visit a friend, Winfield Scott Stratton, in Colorado Springs.

Stratton had left his home in Jeffersonville, Indiana, in 1869, bound for the rich Colorado gold strikes he had read about. When he finally arrived in Colorado Springs in August 1870, twenty-one year old Stratton was nearly broke.16 Stratton applied his carpentry skills he had learned from his father, Myron, to earn a living in those early years in Colorado. By 1873, Stratton's carpentry business was doing well, and he took on a partner, Robert W. Grannis, who happened to be the brother of Dr. John Grannis, Bob Womack's mining partner. Of the many homes Stratton built in Colorado Springs, one was later owned by Helen Hunt Jackson. The new partners ran an ad in the September 21, 1873, issue of the *Weekly Gazette* newspaper which read:

"Grannis and Stratton Contractors, Carpenters and Builders Pikes Peak Avenue Near Nevada Avenue Colorado Springs, Colorado Contracts Taken And Designs Furnished"

Three years later, after learning of the fabulous silver wealth at Leadville, Stratton left Colorado Springs, prospecting at California Gulch, as well as Fryer Hill above Leadville. Disgruntled and discouraged, Stratton left Leadville. Before returning to his home in Colorado Springs, Stratton went to Golden where he enrolled in metallurgy classes at the Colorado School of Mines.[17]

Returning to Colorado Springs, Stratton continued his mining education with Professor Lamb's metallurgy classes at Colorado College. As Lamb was a good friend of Bob Womack's, perhaps this is when Womack and Stratton first met. In any case, it was from Lamb's classes that Stratton learned of the Hayden Survey's findings, and of the "volcanic formation" theory comprising the Cripple Creek region.

At Bob Womack's urging, in that summer of 1891, Stratton agreed to take a look at the prospects of the Cripple Creek District. On a cold day in late May, Stratton arrived at Womack's cabin in Poverty Gulch. Stratton spent a week with Bob, who was happy to show his friend around his beloved mining district. Bob took Stratton from Poverty Gulch east to Gold Hill, on to Bull Hill, and south to Battle Mountain, approximately three miles from Bob's cabin. During that week with Womack, Stratton staked a few claims, including the Washington, and the Vindicator claims.

Stratton gathered a few samples from each claim, and he and Bob made their way back to Poverty Gulch. Along the way, Stratton stopped at a little stream at the base of Battle Mountain, where he happened to spot what he believed to be gold-bearing float, much like Womack had found back in May 1878 at the Womack homestead. Stratton took samples, and staked another claim. As the date of this find was July 4, 1891, Stratton named his claim the Independence. With his ore samples, Stratton left the district and headed back to Colorado Springs. When the samples from the mines assayed lower than Stratton had expected, he leased the Washington and Independence mines.

Coincidentally, it was during this same time that Count Pourtales was also surveying the Cripple Creek District at the invitation of Ed De LaVergne. At the suggestion of George Carr, Pourtales rode over to Poverty Gulch to meet Bob and asked if he would guide him and Thomas Parrish around the mining district. Bob was happy to guide the potential investor around the mining district, taking Pourtales to the same areas he had showed Stratton. At the northern slope of Bull Hill, Pourtales was particularly interested in the Buena Vista mine, owned by Stephen Blair, a carpenter colleague of Stratton's. Pourtales, like Stratton, staked a few claims, gathered some samples, and returned to Colorado Springs.

Two weeks later, the *Weekly Gazette* reported the sale of the Buena Vista mine to none other than Count James M. Pourtales. The purchase price, the paper reported, was eighty thousand dollars. The newspaper reporter, Hiram Rogers, wrote that Pourtales claimed there was nearly a million dollars worth of ore practically in "plain sight," and that there were "at least" a dozen claims in the Cripple Creek Mining District just like the Buena Vista. Apparently, the word of the esteemed Count Pourtales carried more weight with the reporter, than actual ore samples of Bob Womack's claim, and a verified assayer report, which Dr. Grannis had shown Hiram Rogers. In any case, the news of the sale for such an exorbitant amount of money quickly made headlines across the state. Before the end of the summer of 1891, a new influx of prospectors, investors, mining engineers and businessmen had converged in the Cripple Creek Mining District.

With this new influx of prospectors and investors arriving in the district that busy summer, Bob Womack's service as a guide around the mining district was in high demand. Colorado Springs realtor, Charles Tutt, asked Bob to guide him through the region. Tutt and Womack ended up back at Poverty Gulch, where Tutt staked a claim approximately a half-mile north of Womack's El Paso Mine above the gulch. Filed on December 29, 1891, Tutt named his mining claim the C.O.D. Mine. (Cash on Delivery) Bob also showed J. R. McKinnie around the area of

Battle Mountain, where McKinnie staked a claim he called the Mount Rosa Placer. Bob also took Samuel Strong over to Battle Mountain, where he staked the Strong mining claim. Two friends of Bob's from Colorado Springs, volunteer firemen James Burns and James Doyle, also arrived in the district. The two Jimmies asked Bob to show them around. Bob took his friends over to Bull Hill and Battle Mountain. Both Burns and Doyle followed the same practice as everyone else that Bob had taken around the district. Each man staked a few claims, gathered their samples, and returned to Colorado Springs.

William Spell, who served as the recorder for the mining district, received these claims and then would file them with the El Paso County Clerk and Recorders office in Colorado Springs. Spell's son, Leslie Doyle Spell, recalled one such recording incident which indirectly involved Bob Womack:

> "The book work kept him [William] busy as the recording of new claims and properties were located. One recording incident I remember, as dad had quite a time getting the locator straightened out. This man, named E. Porter, called upon dad to record his claim as the 'Gold King.' Dad pointed out to Porter that Bob Womack had already located his claim named the 'Gold King,' Porter cogitated for a few moments and then said: 'Well, then this is the E. Porter Gold King.' Porter's claim was in the vicinity of the Anchoria Leland and Half Moon claims, all of which produced ore for many years." [18]

Meanwhile, the mining towns of both Hayden Placer and Fremont seemed to benefit from stiff business competition. Hayden Placer boasted mercantile and hardware establishments, a blacksmith shop, a laundry service and a restaurant. Because Ed De LaVergne was against alcohol, saloons and gambling houses were all located in Fremont. The first such establishment, housed in a tent, also included a barbershop. The owners were Peter Hettig and Robert Work. They did so well that by the end of that summer they had relocated to a wooden-framed building on the corner of Fourth Street and Myers Avenue.[19] Among the many saloons lining Bennett Avenue were the banking establishments, real estate developers and mining investors. James Parker established the first bank, J. M. Parker's Bank of Cripple Creek. It was housed in the false-front wooden building of A. A. Ireland's real estate business. Doctor A. Hayes, the first physician in the new town, also opened his practice on Bennett Avenue.

Albert A. Carlton and his brother Leslie, arrived in the district from Colorado Springs. The two brothers quickly established their Colorado Trading and Transfer Company which provided freighting services from the district to the nearest railroad depot at Hayden Divide. The first newspaper, the *Cripple Creek Crusher,* printed their first issue on December 7, 1891. The headline was cleverly printed in gold ink. The paper hit the dirt streets of Cripple Creek just hours before the rival newspaper, the Prospector, was printed.[20] With so many new businesses, the realtors Bennett and Myers raised their original fifty dollar lot fee to an incredible two hundred dollars.

New business establishments meant new buildings. Samuel Altman continued to do well with his sawmill and lumber company, even building a second location near the Four Mile area. As families began to move into the town of Fremont, Altman's services were in high demand. Even so, there were no established churches in the new town. Religious services were held every Sunday morning in the back of the Buckhorn Saloon. Bob Womack was often in attendance.

Over the past two years, Hiram Rogers, the reporter for the *Weekly Gazette,* seemed to have developed some sort of angst regarding Bob Womack. Rogers wrote the following article which appeared in the January 16, 1892, issue of the paper:

"Robert Womack is given the credit of discovering the Cripple Creek Mining district, but this is not exactly true. Last winter he found the first rich specimens of ore and brought them into notice, but long before that day the country including and surrounding Cripple Creek had been located in a mining district. From Mr. Robert H. Magee, mail carrier at the postoffice, [sic] I get the following details of the first mining done in that section. It [sic] the latter part of the sixties, Hayden's surveying party passed through this section of country and with them was H. T. Wood. He understood something of mineralogy, and one day picked up a piece of wonderfully rich quartz. He said nothing about it, but in 1874 returned to this country. He told Mr. Magee and others of his find years before, and described the lay of the country. A company was formed to do some prospecting several hundred dollars subscribed, Mr. Magee and others accompanied Wood with a good outfit on a prospecting tour. They got into the mountains from Fountain, up Rock Creek canyon, a route now being urged upon the county commissioners as suitable for a road. Some rich samples of ore were sent to town and a mining excitement followed that was quite as fevered as any that has been known since, considering the population. In the Gazette files of September, 1874, I find the following; 'A miner's meeting, held at Messrs. Coburn & Root's house, on the west branch of Beaver's creek, in El Paso county, territory of Colorado, on the 13th day of August, A. D. 1874, subject to a 'posted notice' call, made by H. T. Wood, R. H. Magee, J. N. Brown, M. E. Jones and A. Coburn. A. Coburn was elected president and H. T. Wood secretary.' "

There are several inaccuracies in Rogers' article, starting with his premise. It is true that Robert Miller Womack did not discover the Cripple

Creek Mining District, he was instrumental in creating it. However Bob Womack was, indeed, without question, by all historic accounts, the man who discovered the rich gold ore that led to the formation of the Cripple Creek Mining District. Further, the Hayden surveying party did not occur in the region during the "sixties." The Hayden surveying team, led by Dr. Ferdinand Vandeveer Hayden during the government sponsored survey of the West, began in 1873, at which time Dr. Hayden hired Bob Womack to guide the surveying team in the Cripple Creek area. While it is true that H. T. Wood was a member of the Hayden survey team by 1874, he could not have discovered the "wonderfully rich quartz" in the "sixties" that Rogers referred to.

However, it is a historical fact that Wood did indeed discover gold-bearing ore during his time with the Hayden Surveying team. Although, as mining engineer and historian Ed Hunter supported the fact, he also wrote:

"The presence of gold on the west side of the Peak was noted in 1874 by H. T. Wood of the Hayden Survey, but little notice was taken of this observation." [21]

Finally, while R. H. Magee's account of the miner's meeting held in August 1874, as reported by Rogers, may be accurate, the establishment of the supposed "mining district" was noted as "subject to a 'posted notice." The El Paso County records show no such filing of said mining district.

Despite the inaccuracies of Hiram Rogers' reporting, Irving Howbert finally decided to check out the Cripple Creek Mining District. Howbert later recalled:

"By the spring of 1892, stories were current in Colorado Springs that mines a few miles southwest of the summit of Pikes

Peak were making carload shipments of a good grade of ore. Even then I was skeptical, thinking that possibly a little surface ore had been found which was not likely to develop into anything of permanent value. I was particularly incredulous because I knew that for ten years Major Demary, an experienced mining man of Park County, had been keeping his cattle on the lands where the gold discoveries were said to have been made, and I reasoned that, if gold in paying quantities existed there, Major Demary surely would have detected it. Later developments showed how badly mistaken I was. Demary's ranch was located in what became the Cripple Creek Mining District, and his house was directly over the very rich and extensive ore bodies of the future Vindicator Mine. Although Major Demary was in the mining business in Park County, he usually spent three or four months on his cattle ranch each year; yet all this time he remained oblivious of the fact that he was living over bodies of ore infinitely richer than any that had ever been discovered in Park County." [22]

Leslie Doyle Spell was ten years old in the summer of 1892. He watched in wonderment as the new town took shape. His father, William Spell, was instrumental in those formidable days. Spell later recounted:

"The gold rush boomed. Towns were incorporated, mayors were elected, and more peace officers were appointed. An assistant for my dad was appointed, a man by the name of 'Hi' Wilson, the 'Hi' possibly a contraction of the name Hiram. Many thrilling tales could be told of this new mining camp. After the influx of the hordes of newcomers to the camp, nothing was too wild or improbable, good or bad. Dad always carried a gun but was never called upon to kill a man, although he could lay them out temporarily if necessary." [23]

The year 1892 brought a frenzy of mining activity unparalleled in Colorado mining history. When W. S. Stratton learned of the incredible amount of money that his friend, Stephen Blair, had received from the sale of his Buena Vista mine, he quickly returned to the Cripple Creek Mining District. After managing to buy back his lease on his Washington claim, Stratton sold it to Count Pourtales' business partner, William J. Wilcox, for eighty thousand dollars, the same amount Pourtales had paid Blair for the Buena Vista mine. Because the Strong mine over on Battle Mountain was also struggling, Sam Strong let it be known around the district that his mine was for sale. Three men, Judge Earnest A. Colburn, Edward Giddings, and William Lennox, pooled their resources, secured a loan and took a sixty thousand dollar option on the Strong mine.

Despite these lower producing mines, prospecting for new claims and development of existing claims continued. Two Colorado Springs pharmacists, A. D. Jones and J. K. Miller, filed a claim, approximately just west of Pourtales' newly purchased Buena Vista mine, on Bull Hill. The two men appropriately named their claim the "Pharmacist." Their ore samples assayed at an astonishing five hundred dollars to the ton.

Prospectors, mine owners and investors suddenly went into a mining frenzy. More mines were located, including the Isabella, Lillie, and the Lone Star, to name a few. While W. S. Stratton received regular payments from his leased Independence mining claim, Stratton began to invest his resources into his reclaimed Washington mine. The two Jimmies, Burns and Doyle, were also developing their mining claims. On a bitter cold day, January 22, 1892, Burns and Doyle found what they believed to be gold-bearing ore on Battle Mountain, above Stratton's Independence mine. The Colorado Springs firemen registered their claim with the El Paso County clerk's office. They called it the "Portland."

Local mining engineers and mining experts across the country, all of whom had a considerable amount of experience in underground mining, now began to assess the viability of the district's production.

That there was ore in the region, they were all in agreement. However, there was disagreement as to how the ore could be separated from its various components. According to one respected local mining engineer, Ed Hunter:

> "One problem with finding gold in the District was that much of the gold was chemically bound with the element Tellurium and miners and investors alike were not familiar with this form of gold." [24]

Despite the seemingly difficulties in the mining process, a determined Bob Womack remained committed in his belief of gold in his beloved Cripple Creek region. Bob continued to work his El Paso mine, producing paying ore, but lacking the funds for transportation to a refining facility. Leslie Doyle Spell later recalled the time when Bob's friends came to his aid:

> "In 1892 when so many of the people were leaving the district, Pourtales, De LaVergne, Andy Frazier, Bob [Womack] and my dad [William Spell] and four of his partners, still had faith and tried desperately to get enough ore to make a shipment from the [mine] figuring that if enough people could see ore actually being shipped, they would remain, with a better chance of incorporating Bob's mine." [25]

Even so, the mining industry was off to a slow but steady start. At the close of 1892, the first full year of mining production in the Cripple Creek District, just over six hundred thousand dollars worth of gold had been produced.

By 1892, there were over two thousand residents in the mining camps. With an ever-growing population and increase of businessmen, investors, and entrepreneurs into the Cripple Creek Mining District, the real estate firm of Bennett and Myers seized the opportunity and promptly raised the fee of business lots to two thousand dollars. Businessmen revolted and chose to locate their establishments at the mining camp of Hayden Placer. It was not long before Bennett and Myers realized the loss of revenue to their competing town. Ed De LaVergne and the other leaders of Hayden Placer also recognized the fact that in their limited plat, the camp could not grow. Therefore, the two competing mining camps of Fremont and Hayden Placer agreed to consolidate.

In an effort of amicable compromise, Bennett and Myers, owners of Fremont, deeded a section of their property which lay against the eastern slope of Mount Pisgah, to the new town to be used for a cemetery. It would be forever known as the "Mount Pisgah Cemetery." [26]

In a unanimous vote, the leaders of both camps voted to name the new mining town, "Cripple Creek," which became official on February 23, 1893. The mayor of Fremont, George Carr, with the help of Bob Womack, who served as Carr's campaign manager, was elected the first mayor of the new town. With a formal municipality in place, the city fathers set about improving the new town. Under Mayor Carr's direction, the first order of business was to have an adequate water and sanitation system installed. Seven telegraph poles were erected and wired for outside communication. Electricity was installed before New York City.[27] Once the beginnings of a real city infrastructure had been put in place, a new rush of entrepreneurs hurried to the Colorado mountain mining camp.

Among the new businesses was Fairley Brothers & Co. Owned and operated by D. B. and C. W. Fairley, the respected Colorado Springs businessmen opened a furniture store on Bennett Avenue. Additionally from Colorado Springs, Ed De LaVergne's family opened their second furniture store on Bennett Avenue. Down the street, a miner's stock exchange, created by local investors and mining experts, also opened. Levi Welty's son, Alonzo, established the Alonzo Welty Livery, Feed and

Stable, at the outskirts of town. [28]

Additionally, Cripple Creek boasted their first church, as well as nearly forty groceries and meat markets, fourteen bakery shops, four department stores, eighty doctors and eight newspapers, and a slew of some twenty-five saloons and gambling establishments. There were also four dance halls, and ten parlor houses. At the lower end of Bob Womack's Poverty Gulch, were over two dozen one-room cribs.

Within three short years of Bob Womack's gold discovery, his beloved region of Cripple Creek had become a viable gold mining district and his Poverty Gulch was now the scene of a thriving business community.

Yet, not even Bob Womack could have predicted what lay ahead.

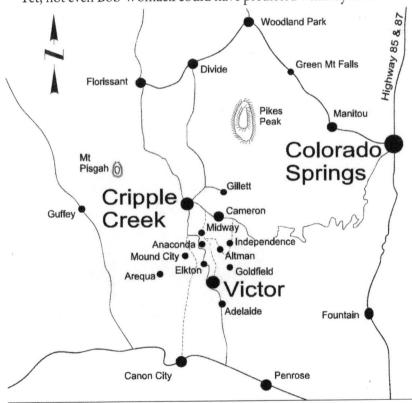

Map of Cripple Creek Mining District. (Courtesy, Paul Marquez)

Fremont was the first mining camp in the District. (Denver Public Library, Western history Department, X-812)

Who's Who of early pioneering men in the District. On horseback is George Carr. William Spell, marshal and friend of Bob Womack, is fourth from the left with tilted hat. Fellow lawman Ed Bell stands in front of the horse. Edward Morton De LaVerne is seated in the doorway next to attorney Charles Adams. (Denver Public Library, Western History Department, X-853)

Bob Womack's Gold King Mine, Bob stands second from left. Ed De LaVerne sits in the wheelbarrow. (Denver Public Library, Western History Department, X-62505)

Bob Womack urged his friend, Winfield Scott Stratton, to stake a few claims in the District. He staked two; the Washington and the Independence, both on the Fourth of July. (Denver Public Library, Western History Department, Z-8875)

Spencer Penrose made millions from his C.O.D. mine. (Denver Public Library, Western History Department, Z-1976)

The Independence made Stratton Cripple Creek's first millionaire. (Denver Public Library, Western History Department, X-62533)

The Portland Mine, owned by Jimmie Burns and Jimmie Doyle would become the richest producer in the District. (Denver Public Library, Western History Department, X-62543)

Chapter 3

The Bowl of Gold &
The Greatest Gold Camp On Earth

The year 1893 started out, literally, with a bang in Cripple Creek. The *Cripple Creek Star* printed the following account in the January 2, 1893, issue:

> "At the stroke of midnight not only did pandemonium break loose in the way of shrieking whistles and booming dynamite and yelling people but also a free flow of free ardent and malt beverages at the different saloons. Despite the commotion, there was very little drunkenness observed and no disturbances."

While the Cripple Creek Mining District "boomed," with activity, there were still non-believers and distracters. Apparently the editor of the Colorado Springs *Weekly Gazette* newspaper was a member this group. The January 23, 1893, issue of the paper included the following editorial:

> "It will take a long time for the district and camp to develop and a good deal of money to find gold at Cripple Creek. Cripple Creek is not a poor man's camp."

Oblivious to the nay-sayers, citizens of the Cripple Creek region had worked to improve the area. Roads in and out of the mining district were critical. One of the first to be constructed was the road between the gold camp and the town of Florissant. J. E. Hundley operated his Hundley Stage Company, complete with six Concord stagecoaches, between the two destination points. The Florence & Cripple Creek Free Road was built along a route in Phantom Canyon. Toll roads were also established between Hayden Divide and the gold camp, as well as from the Cripple Creek Mining District and Canon City, later known as the Shelf Road. [1]

Eleven year old Leslie Doyle Spell spent as much time as he could around the mines in the Cripple Creek Mining District. Years later Spell recounted:

"When a child I would much rather hang around men than children of my own age. Men and their work held a particular fascination for me. If mother wanted me and I wasn't at hand she knew just where to find me. I was either hanging on the tailgate of an ore wagon, or working - at least trying to work. Watching the men drilling in hard rock with their double jacks enthralled me. They would swing their hammers with a terrific blow, deliberately and slowly. If only I could learn to do that! Or, watching the drivers of the ore wagons, sitting on that high seat and pulling the reins on those beautiful horses - if I could only learn to do that! These ambitions were always uppermost in my childish mind. By the time I became of age I had mastered the art of both." [2]

Among the many miners "drilling in hard rock with their double jacks," as young Spell witnessed, was Bob Womack's old friend, Winfield Scott Stratton. He had returned to the Cripple Creek region to once again work his Independence claim on Battle Mountain. For the past two years Stratton had worked the claim with minimal results. During that time, Stratton had sunk a shaft some eighty feet deep, where he found four crosscuts approximately half-way down the shaft. With what ore he was able to break free, Stratton paid for the needed supplies to continue working his claim. However, by 1892, a frustrated Stratton had offered to lease the Independence for five hundred dollars, but no one was interested. Then, after the sensational mining activity in late 1892, Stratton decided to work those crosscuts in his mine one last time.

Leslie Doyle Spell enjoyed following Stratton around the mining district as much he did with Bob Womack. Spell later recalled one such time he and his brother Oakley were with Stratton:

"I, as usual, trailed Mr. Stratton and found it most fascinating to watch him using his magnifying glass as he examined the specimens he found. Stratton was on top of a small shaft using a windlass. The shaft was about 35 feet in depth that time and we could look down into it and see a man working, loading ore into a bucket. While we were there Stratton hoisted the bucket loaded with ore. When he emptied it there was one rock about the size of a water pail. I remember Stratton saying: 'Now, Tom, that's the gold, that stuff that looks like white iron, but that's gold.' The rock was plastered with the precious stuff! Stratton and his partner had sighted [sic] across the alluvial fan where there was no sign of a vein, sunk the shaft through waste material and landed on top of a vein with a rich pocket of ore. The ore soon played out and the partner became discouraged so Stratton bought him out, but continued on. This was the inception of the famous Independence Mine ." [3]

By the summer of 1893, Stratton did indeed give up, returning to Colorado Springs and began looking for someone to lease his Independence mine. Stratton's frustration was not without merit. Professor Duane A. Smith, Colorado historian, described the situation at the Cripple Creek Mining District:

> "There had been no other gold district like this in Colorado. Located in a 10,000-acre bowl of volcanic rock that had been fragmented by eruptive explosions, Cripple Creek showed little surface gold. The ore veins, relatively narrow and not marked by quartz outcroppings, were not sufficiently different from surrounding rock to draw attention. Veins could be discovered only by blasting into the ground or sinking a test shaft." [4]

Finally, Stratton found an investment group to lease his Independence mine. Stratton's terms were five thousand dollars down, with a thirty-day option. L. M. Pearlman, who represented a San Francisco, California, firm, accepted Stratton's terms and wired the check to Stratton's Colorado Springs bank in June 1893. What followed after the lease transaction of Stratton's Independence mine is perhaps one of the most incredible legendary accounts in Colorado mining history.

Stratton returned to the Independence, for what he thought would be the last time. After he had gathered together his tools and supplies, Stratton climbed down the shaft to collect whatever may have been left. At one of the crosscuts he had long since deemed worthless, something caught his eye. Grabbing a pick, Stratton began poking in the center of the crevice. In short order Stratton had managed to break free enough rock that a wide vein of the coveted discolored ore became visible. For the rest of that afternoon, Stratton worked to trace the source of the vein. It was the first of July, 1893, two years almost to the day that he had staked the claim.

Stratton now faced an enormous dilemma. He had three long weeks left on his thirty-day lease with the San Francisco investment firm. After gathering samples, Stratton replaced as much of the rock as possible, hoping Pearlman's crew would not check that particular crosscut. [5]

Back in Colorado Springs, Stratton discreetly took his samples to his old professor, Henry Lamb, at Colorado College. Lamb assayed the ore at an astonishing three hundred and eighty dollars to the ton. After eighteen years as a part-time prospector, forty-two year old Stratton had finally found his gold strike.

For the next few weeks, while Stratton contemplated the possibilities of such a find, he also revisited the "bowl of gold" theory with the professor. The theory, as it was described, reasoned that there were rich veins of ore deposited from the volcano formation, located in the heart of the Cripple Creek region. Or, as retired Adjunct Professor of Geology at Emporia College, Steven W. Veatch, wrote:

> "The Cripple Creek Mining District is centered on a small, circular-shaped, 32.7 million-year-old volcanic complex that covers just over 18 square kilometers (7 square miles.) The complex is centered by Precambrian rocks (quartz and granite.)" [6]

The "volcanic complex" was exactly what Stratton found. This, in essence, was the "bowl of gold" volcanic theory that Stratton had come to believe in, ever since Bob Womack brought him to the Cripple Creek region.

After an agonizing three weeks, Stratton and Pearlman met for dinner in Cripple Creek. It was the night before the thirty-day lease option on the Independence mine, when the two dined at Cripple Creek's popular Palace Hotel. Following their casual dinner, Stratton and Pearlman moved to the hotel lobby, where they enjoyed a cigar near the fireplace.

Pearlman was the first to bring up the subject of the lease on the Independence mine. Pearlman proceeded to tell Stratton of the difficulties his crew were encountering in blasting the granite rock, and the expense of such an operation. While Stratton listened as Pearlman laid out his dilemma, Stratton said not a word. Then, in an unforeseen moment, Pearlman offered to return the thirty-day lease option on the Independence mine back to Stratton. According to Cripple Creek legend, when Pearlman presented the option papers to Stratton, Stratton suggested that Pearlman should throw the papers into the fireplace. Which Pearlman promptly did.

Stratton lost no time in hiring workers to sink more shafts at the Independence mine and began blasting near the rich gold vein. Stratton approached his mining enterprise as he did his carpentry business, calmly and with precision. After his first two ore shipments to the Pueblo smelters had netted him nearly ten thousand dollars, Stratton held ore production to a two thousand dollar daily limit. In this way, Stratton used his rich mine as an investment in his future and the Independence became his own personal bank. Nevertheless, with these production numbers, the Colorado Springs Gazette newspaper would declare Winfield Scott Stratton the first millionaire from Bob Womack's Cripple Creek Mining District. The headline on the front page of the December 26, 1893 issue of the *Gazette* read, "Winfield Scott Stratton Well-known Carpenter Counts his Worth in Seven Figures." Meanwhile, James F. Burns and James Doyle had been working their Portland claim on Battle Mountain, located approximately seven miles from Bob Womack's Poverty Gulch.

Battle Mountain, at an elevation of ten thousand three hundred feet, was situated between Squaw Mountain to the south, and Raven Hill, to the northwest, where Ed De LaVergne had staked a claim. The Portland claim, located several feet above Stratton's Independence mine, sat on just one tenth of an acre. It was surrounded by a jigsaw puzzle of mining claims, many of which crisscrossed over others. It was amidst this quagmire that the two Jimmies worked feverishly to discover a rich vein of ore just as Stratton had. And then it happened. In the early summer of 1893, not long after Burns and Doyle had sunk their first shaft, the men found their gold strike. It was a fine streak of telluride which assayers reported the samples as containing twenty-five percent gold.[7] In effect, the Portland mine was just as rich, possibly richer, than Stratton's Independence mine. The two Jimmies now faced their own mining dilemma.

Burns and Doyle told no one of their rich gold strike. For months they secretly took their ore out of the mine under the cover of darkness. Not trusting transporters, they personally took the ore to the Pueblo smelters. In short order, they had netted over eighty thousand dollars. Both Jimmies agreed they had a fabulous gold vein. Their problem was two-fold. First was the size of their claim. At only one tenth of an acre, there was no room to sink a second shaft. Second, Burns and Doyle were sure their gold vein went through other claims. They needed to find the source of the vein and buy out the adjacent claims. Knowing lawsuits would follow once word of the rich ore vein was out, the two men also needed money.

As W. S. Stratton's Independence mine, just below the Portland mine, was the richest mine on Battle Mountain, the two Jimmies decided to ask Stratton for his help and advice. Stratton readily agreed that Burns and Doyle would be sued under the Apex mining laws. Under the law of Apex, the owner of a claim had to prove ownership of a "mineral vein" to where it reached the surface, or the apex.

After Stratton looked over the Portland mine, the shaft, and the gold vein, he sensed an opportunity. Stratton felt that the rich Portland gold vein had to be a continuation of his ore vein. If he was right, nearly all of Battle Mountain was a gold mine bonanza. Stratton also knew that by the location of the gold vein, and the proximity of his Independence mine almost directly below, he had the best chance of apexing the Portland claim. [8]

Therefore, after much discussion, Burns, Doyle and Stratton agreed to become equal partners in the Portland claim, with Stratton providing the funds for legal fees. Leslie Doyle Spell later commented on the proximity of the ore vein as well as the possibility of millions of dollars worth of gold.

"The prospect on the mountainside near Stratton's became the Portland mine which produced millions in gold bullion, not 'gold brick' as bullion is sometimes mistakenly termed. I am always amused when I hear or read the term 'gold bricks' used when referring to a bonafide product of mining. This find is what touched off the second and largest boom in the Cripple Creek Mining District. Also this is the discovery that eased the financial pressure on the state of Colorado during the panic of 1893. Colorado history was definitely in the making!" [9]

While Stratton hired a group of Colorado Springs attorneys to prepare for the lawsuits sure to come, he sent his most trusted employee, John Harnan, up the mountainside to work with Burns and Doyle. Under Harnan's direction, Burns and Doyle continued to blast, for ore, stockpiling as much ore and cash as possible. It was during this time Colorado's mining industry suffered a heavy economic blow. In 1890, the Sherman Silver Purchase had been passed by the United States Congress and signed into law by President Benjamin Harrison. This act allowed for a larger percentage of silver, rather than gold to back the United States monetary system. The United States Treasury Department was now required to purchase four and a half million ounces of silver per month. As the rich silver mines across the western United States, including Colorado, benefited from the Sherman Silver Purchase of 1890, the silver mines of the West were also an incredible boost to the United States economy. Colorado's silver mining camps of Aspen, Leadville and Creede suddenly became the backbone of Colorado's economy. After the Sherman Silver Purchase Act was passed, the *Creede Candle* editorialized in the January 14, 1891, issue:

> "Certain it is, no other camp yet opened in Colorado could show six as rich producing mines as those opened within eight months from the time the first real intelligent prospecting was done."

Indeed, within a few short months the price of silver rose from forty-eight cents an ounce to an astonishing one dollar and seven cents. However, by 1892 when news of Bob Womack's Cripple Creek gold strike had made the headlines, Colorado's two senators, Henry Teller and Edward Wolcott, attempted to bring about legislation that would make the monetary backing an equal percentage between silver and gold. It soon became a heated debate. On April 20, 1892, Henry Teller, in a speech on the senate floor, said the following:

> "We have fallen upon evil times. We have felt the great power, the tremendous influence of political and partisan attachments and political and party relations. I may be a fanatic, I may be an enthusiast. Every word I have uttered upon this subject lies close to my heart. I warn my party, it can not afford to put itself on the side of a contradiction to the extent of one-half the volume of the money of the world." [10]

In a sense, Senator Teller proved to be correct. As the politicians continued to debate the issue, businesses across the country, not to mention the mining industry, were beginning to feel the uncertainty from the federal government. Fearing an economic recession, many of these businesses began to lay off their employees. Then, in early 1893, when the nation's gold reserve fell below the one hundred million dollar threshold, American citizens began to panic. As the gold reserve continued to dwindle, the country fell into the worst economic depression in history to date.

President Grover Cleveland, who had just been inaugurated as the twenty-fourth president of the United States, felt that the economic crisis was due solely because of the Sherman Silver Purchase Act, passed in 1890. He urged Congress to introduce a bill to repeal the Act, thereby raising the price of gold and correcting the monetary system. The congressional debate would go on for months. Meanwhile, the country was in an economic free-fall. The first quarter report for the year 1893, released by the Colorado Bureau of Labor Statistics, contained the following opening statement:

"From the beginning of the existing financial depression, we have all been more or less impressed with a sense of the wide-spread devastation being wrought in our state through the prostration of an industry which has filled our otherwise solitary mountains with thousands of our bravest and most stalwart citizens, who have built road-ways along the dizzy heights and amidst the awful grandeur of nature's work in her sternest mood."

The report went on to list the unemployment statistics, as well as mining closures for that first quarter of 1893. Aspen reported fifty mines closed, and two thousand unemployed. Leadville reported the same amount of unemployed and ninety closed mines. From Ouray to Silverton and Telluride, the reports were similar. Shortly after the release of such dismal unemployment numbers, newly elected Governor Davis H. Waite spoke at the annual convention of the nationally organized Silver League, held in Denver, on July 11, 1893. Waite closed his speech with a paraphrased section of Revelations 14:20 found in the Bible. Governor Waite said:

"The war has begun. It is the same war which must always be waged against oppression and tyranny to preserve the liberties of man. It is better, infinitely better, that blood should flow to the horses' bridles rather than our national liberties should be destroyed." [11]

Many journalists in the Denver area interpreted Governor Waite's words as a call for revolution. Headlines in the Denver newspapers carried the moniker "Bloody Bridles Waite," which stayed with the governor for the rest of his term. The economic situation grew worse for the country, and newspaper headlines only added to the anxiety Americans already felt. The *Rocky Mountain News* was a perfect example. Under the headline, "Banks Fell Sort of Cash," the July 18, 1893, issue of the paper reported:

"By Agreement Three Savings Banks Fail to Open Doors The Colorado Savings Bank, People's Savings bank and Rocky Mountain Dime and Dollar Savings bank assigned yesterday. It was evident that the depositors, almost without exception, would not listen to reason or argument, and that all realized assets would be exhausted before their demands could be satisfied. Were the banks to suspend during a rush while a crowd of depositors was clamoring at the counter, scenes of disturbance might arise, and this the banks determined to avoid."

The following day, the *Rocky Mountain News* ran another story, a bit more upbeat, on page two, under the headline, "Currency Is Scarce." The article read in part:

"The financial storm broke upon Denver with full force yesterday. A few of the weaker institutions fell before it, but the solid banks stood nobly and there is every reason to believe that the worst is past. In spite of the excitement it can truthfully be said that there was nothing approaching a panic."

Then, as now, Colorado newspapers, with the *Rocky Mountain News* at the forefront, ran cartoons slanting the dire economic situation to fit their narrative. One such cartoon in the July 20, 1893, issue of the *Rocky Mountain News* featured a bank patron at the cashier window being denied a withdrawal, while stacks of bagged cash lined the walls. The many unemployed citizens of Colorado were not amused.

Finally, in August 1893, Congress passed the bill repealing the Sherman Silver Purchase Act of 1890. While President Cleveland got his wish, it was exactly what Colorado senators Teller and Wolcott were fighting against. In effect, the repeal of the Sherman Silver Purchase Act created further economic depression. Almost overnight, silver mines closed and communities were thrown into the already overwhelming crisis of the mass unemployment felt across the country. Of the many who lost their fortunes from silver, was Leadville's Horace Austin Warren Tabor.

Many of Colorado's unemployed miners flocked to the rich gold fields of the Cripple Creek Mining District. The Colorado Springs *Gazette* covered the story and actually interviewed Bob Womack. When asked how the economic depression was effecting the Cripple Creek Mining District, Womack replied, "Cripple Creek's gold will solve the depression." [12]

In a short amount of time, Womack would be proven to be correct. A leading investment firm in Colorado Springs, J. W. Proudfit & Co., issued a statement regarding their view of the repeal of the Sherman Silver Purchase Act:

"Upon the closing of the mints to silver free-coinage, Colorado suffered a severe panic, and many of her friends thought that a still greater disaster would follow the repeal of the silver clause in the Sherman Act. Cripple is ripe for an impetus of this kind and has profited by it to the fullest extent. We venture to assert that it is now one of the main factors, if not actually the most important, in the reviving prosperity of this state, which already is in a much easier financial condition than most of her eastern sisters."

During the summer of 1893, with so many unemployed miners, Stratton was able to hire a second crew to work his Independence mine. In this manner, Stratton began producing high-grade ore nearly twenty-four hours a day. Burns and Doyle hired over two dozen miners. Two shifts worked the Portland mine while another crew hauled wagonloads of ore at night to the Colorado Midland train depot at Hayden Divide. Burns, Doyle and Stratton, in their new partnership, wanted to keep the gold-bearing vein a secret as long as possible. Burns, Doyle and Stratton were able stockpile as much cash as possible, in an effort to hold off the Apex lawsuits sure to come. By the fall of 1893, when news of the rich Portland gold strike became public, the three partners had accumulated nearly three hundred thousand dollars.

When the local press learned of the rich gold vein deep in the crevices of the Portland mine and the possible connection with Stratton's gold vein which had assayed at three hundred and eighty dollars to the ton, there was no longer any doubt as to riches of the Cripple Creek Mining District. Cripple Creek, the press declared, was the "Greatest Gold Camp on Earth."

New investors and entrepreneurs descended on Cripple Creek. David Halliday Moffat, Denver banker and railroad tycoon, opened the Bi-metallic Bank on Bennett Avenue. Spencer Penrose came over the pass from Colorado Springs to join his childhood friend, Charles L. Tutt, in his business ventures. While Penrose became Tutt's equal partner in the C.O.D. mining venture, the two men also opened a real estate business together. Penrose moved into the log cabin of William H. "Harry" Leonard, a fellow bachelor, located at 113 Prospect Street. The firm of Tutt & Penrose invested in various real estate and mining ventures, in the Cripple Creek Mining District, and was one of the first in the district to promote, buy and sell mines. Tutt was one of the earliest investors, having staked the C.O.D. mine in Poverty Gulch, two years previously. The two partners opened their first office at 335 Bennett Avenue, the center of commerce in Cripple Creek. The wooden sign in front of the wooden frame structure read, "Town lots, real estate, mines, and mining stock."

Almost immediately, Tutt and Penrose enjoyed a brisk business. Investors began buying up smaller mining claims and larger mine owners bought adjacent mines. David Moffat bought the Victor mine on Bull Hill. James J. Hagerman bought the Isabella mine. Ed De LaVergne bought a few mines on Raven Hill. Sam Strong, who had previously sold his Strong mine, used the services of Tutt & Penrose when he attempted to purchase another mine. However, Strong had difficulty acquiring the financial backing. No doubt, David Moffat's Bi-metallic Bank also benefited from the many mine purchases.

With all their success in real estate and mining deals, Tutt and Penrose were having very little success with their C.O.D. mine. Discouraged, the two partners leased the mine, for twenty thousand dollars, to Peter Burke and Joseph Troy. The two partners must have been stunned when Burke eventually struck a rich ore vein. However, because Tutt and Penrose still retained ownership in the mine, they shared in the dividends.

In November 1893, no less than forty-seven lawsuits were filed in El Paso County against the owners of the Portland mine, Burns and Doyle. The lawsuits were filed by owners of the Baby Ruth, Hidden Treasure, and Scranton mines, to name a few. Perhaps the largest lawsuit filed against the Portland was that filed by the owners of the Battle Mountain Gold Mining Company.

The president of the Battle Mountain Gold Mining Company, Ebenezer Smith, was a founding stockholder and the first director of the First National Bank of Denver, established in 1860. Coincidentally, David H. Moffat, mine owner and director of Cripple Creek's Bi-metallic Bank, had also become a stockholder and director of the First National Bank of Denver in 1865.

During his time as director of the First National Bank of Denver, Ebenezer Smith, in partnership with Jerome Chaffee, opened a stamping mill in Gilpin County, and developed several gold lodes in the "Richest Square Mile on Earth," including the rich Bobtail lode, where the partners erected the largest ore reduction plant in Colorado Territory at the time. [13]

With his banking background and mining experience, as president of the Battle Mountain Gold Mining Company, Ebenezer Smith, brought the full force of his backers against the owners of the Portland mine. And there were plenty of backers. Included in the Battle Mountain Gold Mining Company, were the gold mines of Anna Lee, Captain, Doubtful, National Belle, and White House. All of these mines were situated near, around, above and below the Portland mine. [14]

The attorneys fighting the lawsuits on behalf of the Portland mine owners, Burns and Doyle, retained by their partner, W. S. Stratton, were well prepared. Allen T. Gunnell and Clarence C. Hamlin, immediately filed counter lawsuits. While Stratton wasn't necessarily opposed to this strategy, he knew it would take years of litigation, with no guarantee of a favorable outcome.

Stratton hired Verner Z. Reed, who not only had a background in mining, but also had recently started his own real estate developing business in Colorado Springs. Reed proved to be a genius at outmaneuvering Ebenezer Smith and the Battle Mountain Gold Mining Company. Reed offered a lease option on the Portland mine to a Colorado Springs associate, Walter Crosby, for two hundred fifty thousand dollars. By Crosby's acceptance of the lease offer, ownership of the Portland remained a "gray area" until such time the lease either ran out, or Burns and Doyle reclaimed possession of the mine. In this way, Reed had effectively tied the hands of the lawyers for the Battle Mountain Gold Mining Company, as there was no one to sue.

Next, Reed, with Stratton's money, began buying the smaller mining claims surrounding the Portland claim. As the mine purchases increased, so did the land holdings on Battle Mountain. Burns and Doyle's original one-tenth of an acre, increased to one hundred eighty acres. With such leverage, Stratton's attorneys, Gunnell and Hamlin, now were in the position to counter any lawsuits by claiming "prior rights" under the law of Apex, in which the owner of a claim had the burden of proof of ownership of a "mineral vein" to where it reached the apex, or surface.

Despite the strategic maneuvers Stratton's men successfully employed, the attorneys for the Battle Mountain Gold Mining Company continued with their lawsuit against the Portland mine. As the case was about to go to court, Stratton's lawyers successfully negotiated a settlement, which cost Stratton, Burns and Doyle two hundred and fifty-thousand dollars. A costly sum indeed. However, Verner Z. Reed, through his many mining claim purchases, had accumulated additional wealth for Stratton,

Burns and Doyle. Thus, he was able to buy out the Battle Mountain Gold Mining Company. While Stratton's attorneys were litigating on behalf of the Portland mine owners, Stratton hired a Cripple Creek attorney, Jonah Maurice Finn, to work strictly for him. Finn was instructed to purchase as many claims adjoining Stratton's Independence mine as possible. At the same time Reed was buying adjoining claims around the Portland mine, Finn managed to purchase eleven claims, surrounding Stratton's claims. When all the lawsuits had been settled, and additional mining claims purchased, Stratton, Burns and Doyle had achieved their goal, the three men now effectively owned nearly all of Battle Mountain.

By the end of 1893, Cripple Creek's gold production rose to over five million dollars. Bob Womack's proclamation that "Cripple Creek's gold will solve the depression," indeed proved to be true.

Early in 1894, Reed dissolved the Battle Mountain Gold Mining Company, and established the Portland Gold Mining Company. Reed went a step further when he offered three thousand shares of stock in the new company. The Portland Gold Mining Company became the first mining company in the Cripple Creek Mining District to register with the New York Stock Exchange. Within a few short months, the company's stock shares soared to an incredible amount of ninety dollars per share. Because of the foresight of the city of Cripple Creek officials, the seven telegraph poles erected in 1892, became quite useful for Cripple Creek's first stock exchange, the Cripple Creek Stock Board and Mining Exchange. This allowed daily information of trading transactions to be wired to Colorado Springs, Pueblo, and Denver, where they were sent on to the New York Stock Exchange. [15]

It was only natural that other mining companies aspired to achieve the same status. Several investors, including Claire Frisbee, the wife of Fred Frisbee, Ed De LaVergne's friend and mining partner, formed a mining company and began buying small and seemingly unprofitable mining claims. Due to her involvement, Claire Frisbee became the second female miner in the Cripple Creek Mining District.

Bob Womack's El Paso mine at Poverty Gulch was one of the many mines absorbed by the new mining company. Both Womack and his partner, Dr. John Grannis, sold their claim to the company, but retained three percent interest of the profits. In honor of Bob Womack's earlier gold discoveries which ultimately led to the "Greatest Gold Camp on Earth," the company was named the Gold King Mining Company. Leslie Doyle Spell later recalled Bob Womack's involvement:

> "Bob [Womack] became discouraged with his mining in the Cripple Creek. A group of men promoted the Gold King, incorporated and gave Bob a block of stock. They installed a fine plant of machinery; built a shaft house, also ore storing house; sunk a shaft several feet deep." [16]

While Bob Womack remained in the Cripple Creek region, living at his cabin at Poverty Gulch, he enjoyed his newfound freedom away from the financial worries of mine development. Perhaps, after years of searching, Bob had finally realized his dream of finding gold which had become a reality and his beloved Cripple Creek Mining District was now the region of the greatest gold rush in America's history. As a quiet, humble man, it is likely that Bob Womack, while knowing he had been credited with that first gold discovery, never took advantage of his status as the discoverer of Cripple Creek's gold. When Bob found the gold float back in 1891, there were less than five hundred residents in the Cripple Creek region. In 1894, the population had soared to over ten thousand. [17]

As the year 1893 came to a close, millionaires by the ore load were made by Cripple Creek's gold. Stratton, the first Cripple Creek millionaire from his rich Independence mine, continued to reap huge profits. The two Jimmie's, Burns and Doyle, became millionaires not only from their fabulously rich Portland mine, but also from the stock dividends from their Portland Gold Mining Company. Horace W. Bennett and Julius Myers, ultimately credited with the consolidation of the mining camps of Fremont and Hayden Placer, also became millionaires from their exorbitant town lot fees.

The gold production from Womack's Cripple Creek Mining District was in the tens of millions. And the new year promised to be even better. In 1894, the C.O.D. mine became another in the growing list of Cripple Creek mines that were producing large amounts of high-grade ore. Womack's friends, Charles L. Tutt and Spencer Penrose, had finally struck a second rich vein at their C.O.D. mine. It was this mining claim that Womack had helped Tutt stake near his own El Paso mine at Poverty Gulch, back in the spring of 1891.

During the panic following the repeal of the Sherman Silver Purchase Act, Tutt and Penrose bought back their lease option on their mine from Peter Burke and Joseph Troy. That same year, Tutt and Penrose, along with W. H. MacNeill and W. H. Leonard, established the Colorado Reduction and Refining Company, located at the mining camp of Lawrence, in the southern end of the mining district. The *Philadelphia Inquirer*, the hometown newspaper of both Penrose and Tutt, printed an article on the front page of the paper, under the auspices of hometown boys finding financial success. The article, appearing in the April 29, 1894, issue of the paper, read:

> "The story of the C.O.D., a private mine owed by five men, and one of the richest strikes in the camp, is hard to credit. In December 1891 Mr. Charles Tutt teamed it over the dangerous Cheyenne route to make a review of the young mining town. At Cripple Creek he met a friend, [Bob Womack} and with him started over the mountains-called "hills." At noon they had reached the Poverty Gulch district and just opposite the Gold King claim. They brushed away the several inches of snow, and

hauled up a log, sat down to regale the inner man. Tutt suggested they put up a stake at this point, and inscribe their location upon it, so it was done. Then after their pipes were lighted, Tutt, half in jest, half as 'bluff,' said to his friend 'Old man, I'll give or take $50 for my interest in this C.O.D. location.' The bluff didn't work, for Tutt's friend was hard up; I'll go you, and sell my interest for $50."

Written with the fine flair of 19th century journalism, the following piece described the ever-nagging problem for the Cripple Creek Mining District, adequate roads.

"While a cow ranch had been maintained for many years in the lower end of what is now the town of Cripple Creek, the only wagon road leading into the ranch was an almost impassable one from the west, leading up and across Four Mile creek, or the one from Florissant. When the first gold excitement broke out in 1891 there was no wagon road and not even a recognizable trail leading into the district from Colorado Springs. In the spring of 1891 a livery man by the name of Johnson, at Florissant, established a kind of make-shift stage line, the first to connect with the new El Dorado. The roads were little more than a trail, the horses used were small cow-ponies, of the balky variety, the stage a spring wagon."

So wrote T. M. Howell, quite possibly Cripple Creek's first historian. [18]

Indeed, transportation into and out of the Cripple Creek Mining District for both visitors and the all important gold-bearing ore was a problem. That all changed with the arrival of the first of many railroads into the district.

On July 2, 1894, Bob must have witnessed the arrival of the first railroad into the Cripple Creek Mining District. All summer long it had been a race between two railroad companies as to which one would be the first to complete their tracks and roll into town.

The owners of the mines, over one hundred and fifty by 1894, were losing profits to the high transportation costs incurred when shipping their ore to smelters. W. S. Stratton approached an old friend, Harry E. Collbran, the general manager of the Colorado Midland Railroad depot at Hayden Divide. Stratton and Collbran agreed that a railroad was needed at the Cripple Creek Mining District. When Collbran's superiors rejected the idea, Collbran, determined to build a rail line into the gold mining district, sought financial backing. Stratton steered Collbran to another acquaintance of his, Colorado Springs millionaire, Harlan P. Lillibridge. With a one hundred thousand dollar loan from Lillibridge, Collbran formed his own company which he named the Midland Terminal Railroad. However, Collbran's railroad crew had only laid nine miles of narrow-gauge track from Hayden Divide before Collbran ran out of the needed funds to continue.

While Collbran tried to secure additional capital, David Moffat was well into the process of building his own narrow-gauge rails from Florence toward the mining district. Moffat's planned Florence & Cripple Creek Railroad would run forty miles. Leaving Florence, rails ran north and then up a steep and winding grade through Phantom Canyon, climbing over five thousand feet. From there, the rails would continue to climb to an elevation of over ten thousand feet before entering Cripple Creek, an elevation of nine thousand five hundred feet. Finally, in the spring of 1894, Moffat's railroad crew began making great strides in their progress. By mid-summer the rail line had been completed. It was a hot day July 2, 1894, nevertheless, nearly all of Cripple Creek's citizens lined both sides of Bennett Avenue to witness the arrival of the first train into their town. It must have been quite a sight, a defining moment for progress. The townfolks would not learn until after the celebrations were over that the last passenger car had jumped the track near the mining camp of Anaconda. Plunging approximately forty feet down an embankment, there was one fatality, that of W. G. Milner. [19] The July 3, 1894 issue of the *Daily Record* reported:

> "Sixty passengers enjoyed the maiden voyage, with the train scuttling along at a breakneck speed of three miles an hour. At the outskirts of Anaconda, the train went of the track and over an embankment. Twenty-one people were injured and one was killed."

Competition between the railroads was soon overshadowed by a new competition between the two largest towns within the Cripple Creek Mining District. Due to the fabulous wealth of the mines on Battle Mountain, dominated by Stratton, Burns and Doyle, a small mining camp, consisting of tents and shanties, quickly sprang up near the southern base of the mountain.

In 1893, Warren Woods, a Denver businessman, arrived in the Cripple Creek Mining District with his sons, Frank and Harry. Looking over the area just south of Battle Mountain intending to develop a townsite, the Woods eventually bought out their competitor, the Mount Rosa Mining, Milling, and Land Company, originally established by J. R. McKinnie. The Woods purchased the entire company for one thousand dollars, a strategic land grab of sorts.

Forming the Woods Investment Company, Woods and his sons laid out a plat for a new townsite. On November 6, 1893, the town of Victor, named for Victor C. Adams, a local homesteader, was officially platted. Frank and Harry Woods marketed town lots for twenty-five dollars, which quickly sold, and businesses were established along the four-block platted townsite.

Marketing these lots as "gold mines" for the perspective merchants turned out to be quite prophetic for the Woods brothers. By early 1894 they had begun construction of a much needed hotel in the growing mining town. During the land-grading, process for the hotel, at the corner of Diamond Avenue and 4th Street, the heart of the mining town, Frank Woods hit a twenty inch vein of gold. Production of the hotel immediately ceased and the Woods brothers traced the vein of gold to the Gold Coin claim, which they quickly bought for a few thousand dollars. A shaft was sunk in the middle of the street, and the Gold Coin Mine was erected on the main thoroughfare of Victor. Following the Woods brothers fabulous gold strike, Victor came to be known as the "City of Mines." For the Woods brothers, their future pay dirt would come from the gold, not the hotel which became an investment, benefiting the Woods and the city of Victor. Within a year, Frank and Harry Woods' Gold Coin Mine was producing fifty thousand dollars a month.

Frank and Harry Woods bought another lot, downhill and a block south, from their original hotel site. Simply called the Victor Hotel, it was built at the southeast corner of Victor Avenue and 4th Street. The showplace of Victor, a technical marvel for the region, featured electricity throughout the building. The corner entrance of the Victor Hotel, at the downslope of 4th Street, boasted enclosed balconies directly above both the second and third floor levels. Three stories high, the Victor Hotel, was the tallest business in town. The opening of the hotel, in July 1894, coincided perfectly with the first completed rail line into the District; The Florence & Cripple Creek Railroad. The *Cripple Creek Journal,* dated July 2, 1894, covered the event:

> "A grand ball will be given at the Hotel Victor, Victor, Colorado, to-night. A special train will leave Cripple Creek at 8:30 p.m. returning after the dance closes. The ball will be one of the most interesting of the season."

Because the Florence & Cripple Creek narrow-gauge railroad was the first to reach the Cripple Creek Mining District, Moffat's company enjoyed an incredible amount of business hauling the district's rich ore to the smelters. It was a win-win business venture for both Moffat and the mine owners. Shipping prices went down, resulting in higher profits for the mine owners.

While Moffat was reaping high profits from the mining district's gold bonanza, Harry Collbran, who had remained in his position as general manager of the Colorado Midland Railroad, managed to secure additional funds and a new partner, W. G. Gillett, fellow employee and company auditor with the company. Collbran and Gillett used their executive authority within their company to use many of the railroad workers to lay rails from the Colorado Midland depot at Hayden Divide, southwest to the gold mining district. For whatever reason, perhaps in an effort to gain an advantage over the competition, Collbran chose to switch from his original plan of narrow-gauge rails to standard-gauge rails. Therefore, the entire nine miles of previously laid track were rebuilt. The rail lines would eventually pass through the small mining towns of Anaconda, Elkton, and Cameron. It was a costly venture; seventy thousand dollars per mile.

Collbran and Gillett knew the richest mines were on Battle Mountain and Bull Hill, close to Victor, not to mention the mines located right in the town. Therefore, their railroad would go directly to Victor. Albert A. Carlton and his brother, Leslie, owned and operated the Colorado Trading and Transfer Company, located on the east end of Cripple Creek's Bennett Avenue. The Carlton brothers believed that with a second railroad serving their town, competition would benefit both the citizens as well as commerce. Therefore, the two men offered Collbran the lot adjacent to their business lot, for the railroad's depot location. In return, the Carlton brothers asked for exclusive rights to deliver freight and ore to the railroad. Collbran agreed to the business proposition. However, because a depot was already under construction at Gillett, named for

Collbran's partner, the idea of a new depot was put on hold. Finally, in December 1895, the standard gauge Midland Terminal Railroad arrived in the Cripple Creek Mining District. Passengers paid two dollars for a round trip ticket. The rail yards for the Midland Terminal Railroad were headquartered at Bull Hill, near the summit of Victor Pass, an elevation of ten thousand feet. The Carlton brothers were soon proven to be correct in their assessment of competition. The Midland Terminal Railroad reaped huge profits from the transportation of freight and gold ore from the Cripple Creek area, thanks to the services of the Carlton brothers. Collbran and Gillett also had a monopoly on the freight business from the town of Victor and the many mines, as the Florence & Cripple Creek Railroad did not actively pursue that business.

Nevertheless, both railroad companies enjoyed a brisk business, particularly the Midland Terminal Railroad Company. Collbran ran four trains daily throughout the Cripple Creek District. Passenger trains arrived and departed three times a day; at 3:30 p.m., 8:30 p.m., and 11:30 p.m. An additional passenger car was available at 2:40 a.m. Pullman service was also available on selected cars. The promotional company of Jno. W. Proudfit & CO., of Colorado Springs, published the following in their January 1894 publication:

"In the early days of the district the cost of transportation and treatment of ore ran from $28 to $35 a ton. It is needless to say that these figures made it impossible to market any but the high grade ores. A few weeks ago by the completion of the Midland Terminal, the distance to be freighted by wagon was reduced. The competition of the railroads and the further stimulus offered by the shortening of the haul, combined with the cut in treatment charges made by rival smelters have made it possible to market ore at a cost of $15 to $18 a ton. With the nearer approach of the railroads this charge will be still further lessened. Had it not been for the financial depression which, in the early part of 1893, made the raising of capital for any purpose almost an impossibility, this state of things would have been remedied long ago. So far back as the summer of 1892 preparations for building a railroad into the camp were in rapid progress and actual construction was started on the Midland Terminal. Nothing could forcibly illustrate the great economic importance of the Cripple Creek district than these active railroad undertakings—involving an outlay of $3,000,000—in this period of general financial depression."

In the spring of 1896, Collbran began building the new railroad depot proposed by the Carlton brothers. Located on the most eastern lot of Bennett Avenue, the new Midland Terminal Depot was a three-story brick building, with one portion of the structure, built lower, due to the uneven land. From the time the new depot opened in the summer of 1896, it became the focal point for Cripple Creek activity. Cripple Creek's citizens would often stop by the Midland Terminal Depot to pass the time of day, enjoying the arrival and departures of the train, and watch the comings and goings of the passengers.

Among those who enjoyed this pastime, was Bob Womack. Bob would often ride his horse, Whistler, down from Poverty Gulch, to the train depot, where he relaxed on a bench and took in the sights of the busy activity.

A month later, Bob Womack would also witness disasters in the heart of his beloved Cripple Creek Mining District.

Horace Bennett, along with Julius A. Myers, platted and established the town of Cripple Creek. (Denver Public Library, Western History Department, F-18332)

Bennett and Myers platted their town, sight unseen, in Denver, Thus the uneven Bennett Avenue was constantly under construction and maintenance. (Denver Public Library, Western History Department, P-937)

It was a big event when the stagecoaches, such as this one, arrived in Cripple Creek. (Denver Public Library, Western History Department, WHJ-789)

Governor Davis H. Waite became known as "Bloody Bridles Waite" for his stance on Colorado's labor and coinage issues. (Denver Public Library, Western History Department, Z-1966)

By 1893 Cripple Creek gold solved the state's economic depression. The Anchoria-Leland is high on the hilltop while Womack's Gold King and Penrose and Tutt's C.O.D. are in the valley below - an example of the "Bowl of Gold" theory. (Denver Public Library, Western History Department, X-62511)

After Bob Womack sold the Gold King Mine it became a large producer. (Denver Public Library, A.J. Harlan photographer, X-62504)

Bob Womack about the time he sold the Gold King Mine but retained stock in the company. (Denver Public Library, Western History Department, F-12175)

David H. Moffat was instrumental in bringing the first railroad into Cripple Creek. He also opened the largest bank in town, the Bi-Metalic. (Denver Public Library, Western History Department, H-123)

The Florence & Cripple Creek Railroad was the first to arrive in the District. (Denver Public Library, Western History Department, MCC-445)

The Midland Terminal Railroad served the many mines in the District by cutting prices. (Denver Public Library, Western History Department. Z-15906)

Chapter 4

The Not So Golden Years

Ever since Bob Womack's gold discovery in 1890, a steady stream of millionaires were made from Cripple Creek's gold. Bob Womack enjoyed spending time with his old friends Winfield Scott Stratton, Spencer Penrose, Charles Tutt, and the two Jimmies, Burns and Doyle. Following Bob Womack's gold discovery in October 1890, it was the mines owned by these men, which Bob had helped to locate. All of these mines were now using the latest mining equipment, and Bob was learning about the new technology. These improvements provided the mine owner the necessary machinery to sink shafts deeper into the hard granite then ever before.

It was due to this advanced technology that Bob Womack's Cripple Creek Mining District remained the "Greatest Gold Camp on Earth." As such, it would also be the last great gold rush of America. Mining engineer, Ed Hunter wrote:

> "Mining in Cripple Creek mirrored the changes that had taken place in the mining industry in the last 100-plus years."[1]

With the advances in hard-rock mining, mines such as the C.O.D., Independence, Mollie Kathleen, and Mary McKinnie were employing hundreds of men. The Portland on Battle Mountain had the most workers, over seven hundred. With so many employed at the various mines, small communities were formed near the larger mines.

Anaconda, named for the mine at the base of Squaw Gulch, grew in size and population. This was due to the arrival of David H. Moffat's Florence & Cripple Creek Railroad, which ran through the town. The town served the larger mines, such as the Vindicator, Mary McKinnie, Morning Glory and the Jack Pot.

Elkton, a smaller mining community, was named for the rich mining claim staked by brothers George and Samuel Bernard. Located midway between Cripple Creek and Victor, Elkton was perhaps the most successful with two drug stores, two doctors, restaurants, hotels and several saloons.

The largest of these mining communities was the small town of Independence, named for W. S. Stratton's Independence mine on Battle Mountain. Shortly after the Independence mine became a rich ore producer, Stratton built a cabin at the base of Battle Mountain near Wilson Creek. While Stratton continued to live in Colorado Springs, he stayed at this cabin during his time in the mining district. It was at this cabin that Bob Womack and W. S. Stratton spent time together, discussing the various aspects of mining.

The mining camp of Independence sprang up in 1895 in the area around the Hull City Placer property. Very quickly, Stratton's Independence Town and Mining Company purchased the land and the mining town was promptly renamed "Independence." Officials of the Independence Town and Mining Company placed advertisements for their new town in the various Cripple Creek newspapers. One such ad read:

"The youngest and most promising town in the great gold

camp. In twelve months it will be the commercial center of the great Cripple Creek District." [2]

The advertisement presented a lofty goal which never was achieved. Even so, with the proximity of the town, near the rich mine producers of the Vindicator to the east, and the adjacent Hull City mine, Independence grew in size, spreading out toward the base of Bull Hill. Within a year, the population of Independence was over two thousand.

Another mining town, which would become a focal point in a dark chapter of Cripple Creek's history, was the town of Altman, established in 1893. The town father, Sam Altman, had previously started the first sawmill business in the district at the base of Womack's Poverty Gulch. Shortly after Stratton had made a success of his Independence mine, Altman staked his own claim, the Free Coinage, on Bull Hill. By 1893, Altman had discovered a rich vein. Not long after, he incorporated his own mining town, which he named, appropriately, Altman. Situated high on a stretch of ground between Bull Hill and Bull Cliff, an elevation of ten thousand six hundred feet, Altman was known as the "highest city in the world." [3] Within a year, Altman opened the first stamp mill in the district, employing nearly a hundred workers. Altman and, in particular, the stamp mill served many of the mines in the area including the Buena Vista, Deadwood, Victor, and the Pharmacist. By 1895, Altman boasted twelve hundred residents, three groceries, two hotels, a boarding house, six saloons and even telephone service. There were over two hundred wooden framed homes, made from lumber supplied by Sam Altman's second sawmill company.

Altman, a strong union labor town, became the center of the labor wars that took place in the Cripple Creek Mining District. Miners were paid a standard wage of three dollars a day for an eight hour work day. However, in 1894, several mine owners had called for a nine hour work day. The superintendent of the Buena Vista mine was the first to increase the daily shift by an hour, with no increase in wages.

The miners were not happy. One miner decided to take action. John Calderwood began his mining career at the age of nine in the mines of his native Scotland. After graduating from the McKeesport School of Mines in 1876, Calderwood emigrated to the United States, eventually finding work in the Pennsylvania coal mines. Later, Calderwood moved west, where he worked in the mines near Butte, Montana. At Butte, Calderwood was involved in a vicious confrontation between mine owners and miners. Following the incident, Calderwood was instrumental in the formation of the miner's union, known as the Western Federation of Miners, which was formalized at Butte, on May 15, 1893.

By 1894, Calderwood was in the Cripple Creek Mining District, working at Sam Altman's Free Coinage mine. When Calderwood learned of the added hour in the miners' work day, he set about organizing the men of the Free Coinage as well as those at the Buena Vista mine, to join the WFM labor organization. In short order Calderwood also got miners from the Poverty Gulch area, Anaconda and Victor, to join the miners' union.

Although the Buena Vista was the only mine to increase the hours, many of the other owners saw the organization of a miners' union as a real threat. In February 1894, the owners, including Sam Altman, David Moffat and James Hagerman joined forces. Backed by the national Mine Owners Association, the owners followed the lead of Buena Vista's superintendent, Bradford Locke, by announcing they would also increase the work day from eight to nine hours, while keeping the daily wage at three dollars. It is interesting to note that neither Stratton, Burns or Doyle raised their work-day hours.

Outraged, Calderwood called for a strike against the mine owners. Five hundred men joined the strike. However, nearly seven hundred miners continued to work in the mines that offered eight-hour work days. With local miners split on the union issue, Calderwood set about converting workers to the union cause. For the those who had joined the strike, Calderwood used union funds to set up a tent city, complete with a mess kitchen.

As the strike went on, tempers on both sides grew short. In March, representatives from the mines went to Colorado Springs and asked Judge John Campbell for an injunction. The owners were seeking to restrain Calderwood and the WFM from interfering with their operations. After Judge Campbell agreed to the injunction, the mine owners returned to the district where they announced they would be hiring "scab" workers.

On March 15, 1894, El Paso County Sheriff, Frank Bowers, arrived in Altman, to serve Calderwood with a restraining order. Calderwood and his group of members from Union No. 19, were based at Sam Altman's Free Coinage mine. Before he returned to Colorado Springs, Bowers agreed to leave six of his deputies in the area to ensure the peace.

Obviously, this did not sit well with members of the miner's union. Before nightfall, the strikers had organized into a mob, forming at the Victor mine around midnight. Noticing the three sheriff deputies, a few of the men surrounded them and took them as hostages. Evidently, Calderwood intervened, as the three deputies were released before the sun rose the next morning.

Nevertheless, the striking miners' mob were not finished. They began harassing and threatening the scab workers. News of the violence erupting in the Cripple Creek Mining District soon made headlines across the state. The *Rocky Mountain News* covered the story in the March 17, 1894, issue, under the headline, "Riot At Altman."

Fearing the Altman situation would only grow worse, Sheriff Bowers asked Governor Davis H. Waite to send troops of the Colorado Militia to the area. Waite, elected on the Populist ticket, and a proponent of the pro-labor movement, obviously had hesitations. Governor Waite's reply to the sheriff included the statement, "calling the troops must be the last resort." Nevertheless, before the day was over, the governor dispatched the requested troops to Altman.

Several companies of the Colorado Militia, under the command of Adjutant General Thomas Tarsney, arrived in the mining district at 6:00 the following morning. Tarsney and his men set up their camp at George Carr's ranch. Tarsney attempted to negotiate a settlement by meeting with both parties, with little success. For the next two months, tempers boiled as both sides were at a stalemate.

In April the striking miners took things too far. Two miners, W. S. Ferguson and William Rabideau, acting as spies for the mine owners, attended a WFM meeting. When their identity was discovered, some of the strikers, led by Jack Smith, kidnapped the two men. At one of the mines, they tortured the men, then shoved Rabideau down one of the shafts. Ferguson was taken to the edge of town where he was left and warned never to return.

One of Calderwood's leaders, Junius J. Johnson, built a log fort at the top of Bull Cliff. Armed sentries stood watch around the clock and others patrolled the area near the mines. The citizens of Altman became alarmed and demanded an end to the strike.

Irving Howbert, former El Paso County Clerk, met with the mine owners. Howbert suggested they get as many El Paso County sheriff deputies as Sheriff Bowers would allow and recruit more, if needed. The mine owners were able to enlist over one hundred El Paso County lawmen to restore order at Altman. Early on the morning of May 25, 1894, lawmen boarded the train at Colorado Springs. At Florence, the men changed trains, riding the rest of the way on Moffat's narrow gauge Florence & Cripple Creek Railroad to Altman.

Calderwood and Johnson had their own spies among the Western Mine Owners Association. As soon as they learned that members of the El Paso County Sheriff's Department were on their way, they spurred their own men into action. The striking miners laid rows of dynamite at the shaft and boiler houses of the Strong mine on Battle Mountain.

At 9:30 a.m., just as the Florence & Cripple Creek train rounded the last curve and headed toward the town of Victor, the Strong mine exploded. As soon as the train stopped at the depot, the El Paso County lawmen rushed to the scene. However, due to the strike, the mine was unoccupied, therefore, no one was hurt. Nevertheless, the owners of the Strong mine, Judge Earnest A. Colburn, Edward Giddings, and William Lennox, were furious. They immediately contacted Governor Waite and demanded he send out reinforcements for the El Paso County lawmen. Instead, Governor Waite told the owners he wanted a peaceful negotiation and would come to the mining district as soon as possible. When the governor arrived on May 26, he wasted no time in issuing the following statement, "Good citizens, lay down all arms and cease all acts in violation of the peace of the state." [4]

Given his stance on pro-labor issues, Governor Waite's first meeting was with the members of the Western Federation of Miners local chapter, Union No. 19, based at Altman's Free Coinage mine. Evidently it was a productive meeting for all concerned, as the leaders of the WFM appointed Governor Waite to be the "sole arbitrator" in the labor strike. It was the first time in Colorado history that a sitting governor was chosen to speak for one side of a conflict, against the other side. [5]

To his credit, Governor Waite agreed to meet the few mine owners who requested a meeting. The meeting was held on neutral ground, at Colorado College in Colorado Springs. After the four-hour meeting ended in a deadlock over a variety of issues, Waite returned to Denver. Meanwhile, violence at Altman continued. Several of the strikers broke through Stratton's guards at his Independence mine and took possession for a short time. Finally, even the Populist governor, Davis Waite, had enough. On June 6, 1894, Governor Waite called for the National Guard to mobilize and prepare to defend the Cripple Creek Mining District. As the governor's troops boarded the train bound for

Altman, Governor Waite sent a wire to El Paso County Sheriff Bowers, which smacked of his true feelings regarding the labor issue.

> "In present excitement I hope you will not advance the deputies. It may result in bloodshed, which can be avoided if time can be given for state troops to reach the field. They are not a lawful body; are only armed marauders, and you must treat them as such." [6]

The following day the governor's troops arrived in Altman. The men strategically placing themselves between the mines and the fortress constructed by Johnson and members of the WFM. A stalemate ensued for days. Finally it was Adjutant General Thomas Tarsney, the founder and leader of the Western Federation of Miners, who elected to meet with the mine owners and bring an end to the strike. A negotiated settlement was reached, whereby the El Paso Sheriff deputies would leave the area, but the governor's troops would remain to ensure the peace.

While this seemed to be an end to the violence, it did nothing to address the original issue of the four month long strike. A group of a dozen disgruntled WFM members resented the action of their leader. The men followed Tarsney to Colorado Springs where he was staying at the Antlers Hotel. There, on June 22, three of the men cornered Tarsney, knocked him unconscious with the butt of a gun and kidnapped him. Placing Tarsney in the back of their hack, the men drove to the edge of town, where they dumped Tarsney's limp body on the ground. Then, the men stripped him of his clothing and proceeded to tar and feather him. [7]

The Cripple Creek labor strike was the longest dispute up to that time. It was also very costly. Over three million dollars was lost in the form of ore production, local business, as well as local and state costs for the militia and National Guard troops.

For Bob Womack, it must have been devastating to witness such senseless activities in his beloved Cripple Creek Mining District. Sadly, Bob would see more tragedy.

In the five years since Womack and his friends had officially formed their mining district, the population had swelled to over thirty thousand people. The 1894 Cripple Creek Business Directory listed nearly eight hundred businesses. With such prosperity, city officials were able to enact many improvements to the growing city. In 1894, a reservoir was completed near a hill, approximately two hundred feet above the city's main street, Bennett Avenue, and the corner of Second Street. A second reservoir was located north of the city, at Third Street and Pikes Peak Avenue. Nearly three miles of underground pipe had been laid from this reservoir to the city's main lines. This not only provided water for the town, it also would provide the needed water should there ever be a fire.

In town, a six hundred pound fire bell was purchased, and water hydrants were installed, Dr. J. A. Whiting was instrumental in the formation of the J. L. Lindsay Hose Company, constructing a hose house on the north end of town, just below the ridge of Golden Avenue. [8]

City officials had also purchased two lots on Bennett Avenue for a fire station, as well as a new city hall. A group of men formed as volunteer firemen. When George Jordan was appointed as the first fire chief, the volunteer force had grown to one hundred and seventy-five men. By the time the brick building on Bennett Avenue was completed, the Cripple Creek fire department had acquired three hose carts, a hook and ladder wagon and a hand-drawn chemical engine.

Unfortunately, all the preparations put in place by the Cripple Creek officials and the fire department could not save the town from the worst fire disaster in its history. The unusually warm spring weather brought gusty winds. Those winds fed a fire that nearly destroyed the town.

At noon on Saturday, April 25, 1896, fire broke out on Myers Avenue and moved from building to building.

Earlier that morning, a young couple, staying in an upper room of the Central Dance Hall, located on the south side of Myers, began to argue. As their argument became physical, the woman, Jennie LaRue, was knocked backward, turning over a gas stove. [9] The spilled flammable liquid spread across the floor engulfing everything in its path. Within minutes the wood-framed structure of the Central Dance Hall was ablaze. Very quickly the fire spread. Fifteen minutes later, firebox number 21 of the newly installed fire alarm system was pulled. [10] The firemen quickly arrived on scene with their hook and ladder wagon, with members of the J. L. Lindsay Hose Company right behind them. The firemen and hose team were able to contain the fire to the south side of Myers Avenue, until one of the two hoses broke. By that time, the area so thick with black billowing smoke, the firemen could barely see and were using wet sponges to breath through. Control of the fire was quickly lost. This may have been due, in part, by the absence of the fire chief, Frank G. May. Sadly, his infant son had died earlier that morning and he was unable to participate. Cripple Creek Police Chief, James M. Marshall stepped in, handling both police and fire duties.

The fire spread, engulfing every building on the south side of the street between Third and Fourth streets. As the south winds began to pick up, sparks from the burning buildings jumped to the buildings on the north side of Myers Avenue. The first to go up in flames was the Topic Theater, owned by Charles Tutt and Spencer Penrose, followed by the Butte Opera House. Within minutes, every dance hall and parlor house on the street were a mass of flames.

In an effort to minimize the spread of the fire and create firebreaks where possible, Police Chief Marshall ordered buildings along Myers and Bennett avenues, to be blown up. Using dynamite, buildings at the corner of Myers Third Street were leveled.

The fire moved north to Bennett Avenue. As the post office began to burn, the workers fled, leaving the mail and the rest of the contents behind. By that time, the firemen and hose team were able to use the high masonry wall, which divided the upper and lower sides of Bennett Avenue between Third and Fourth streets, as a natural barrier for defense. The men placed the hoses on top of and in front of the barrier in an effort to stop the fire from crossing Bennett Avenue. [11] Unfortunately, due to the intense heat and thick smoke, the firemen were forced to retreat. The fire quickly jumped to the north side of the street. Johnny Nolan's Saloon was the first to catch fire. Next, Moffat's First National Bank went up in flames, followed by the Mining Exchange building. When Police Chief Marshall realized the fire would soon engulf the new City Hall building, he and jailer, Tom Ryan, released the twenty prisoners from the locked jail.

Within an hour after the fire began, the smoke could be seen from as far away as Victor. Officials scrambled to assemble their hook and ladder team, while waiting arrival of a special Florence & Cripple Creek train. When the train finally arrived, shortly before 3:00 p.m., the Victor firemen loaded their equipment on the flatbed train car, and climbed aboard. The F. & C. C. left the depot and arrived in Cripple Creek in a record seven minutes.

Victor firemen wasted no time in hooking their twelve hoses to the five fire hydrants in the area of the fire. However, with so many hose lines, including Cripple Creek's two hoses, all hooked up to the same water source, there was very little water pressure to fight the fire. As this situation was being rectified, the fire raged and spread, and spread.

Jim Marshall and his police force, began to evacuate the citizens, who by this time were in a panic. Meanwhile, other members of the police department rounded up every freight and ore wagon they could and began emptying stores of such items as clothing, blankets, canned goods and anything else that might be needed by the citizens in the days after the fire.

The fire spread further north, engulfing everything in its path. Crossing Carr Avenue, destroying the Baptist, Congregational, and

Episcopal churches, before jumping further north to Eaton Avenue. The recently established Sisters of Mercy Hospital, on the south side of Eaton Avenue, barely escaped the fire's wrath. The Sisters wrapped their patients in blankets, taking them to homes west of the area, where, as yet, there was no threat of fire. The Sisters had acted just in the nick of time. Shortly after the evacuation, the fire grew again and moved toward the hospital. Once again, Police Chief Marshall ordered buildings, including several residential homes, to be dynamited, in an effort to impede the spread of the fire. In the process, while the hospital was saved, homes were destroyed. As the sun began to set on that frightening day, the winds had calmed, allowing the fire fighters to finally gain the upper hand. However, it was well after midnight before the firemen's hoses doused the last of the glowing embers of fire. On Sunday morning, town officials, policemen and firemen were assessing the damage to the town. Nearly thirty percent of the town had burned to the ground. Property loss was determined to be half a million dollars. Amazingly, several business owners were already busy rebuilding their establishments. By Wednesday many businesses had reopened, including the First National Bank and the *Cripple Creek Morning Times*, which never missed an issue.

A sense of normalcy seemed to return as Cripple Creek's citizens resumed their everyday lives. That is, until approximately 1:30 p.m. on April 29, 1896, four days later, the sound of the fire bell again rang out. Fire broke out on the northeast corner of Second Street and Myers Avenue, the site of Horace Bennett's wooden-frame Windsor Hotel, built in 1892. The hotel had recently been leased and renamed the Portland Hotel, although the lease negotiations were not yet finalized. This would later fuel wide speculations in the Cripple Creek and Colorado Springs newspapers.

One of the hotel waitresses, Bessie Kelly, discovered the fire racing up the grease-soaked walls of the kitchen. She immediately alerted her husband, C. H. Kelly, the hotel's bartender. While Bessie hurried up the stairs to retrieve what personal belongings she could from their room, C. H. took the cash from the register. All the while, flames were coming from the stovepipe opening causing the fire to spread. Bessie and the other waitresses were nearly trapped upstairs by the fire. Fortunately they made their way down the outside stairway, through the smoke-filled air, to safety.

When the firemen arrived, the entire building was engulfed in flames. Smoke was rolling from under the base cornice of the structure. The firemen used their hoses, sending a steady stream of water on the burning hotel, as well as the alley, but to no avail. At approximately 2:45 p.m., the roof of the Portland Hotel collapsed. The fire was out of control. The fire jumped north, crossing Myers Avenue, with sparks and embers landing on the roof of the Wright Hardware store. Within minutes that building was ablaze. As the fire in the building grew, the ammunition stocked in the store exploded, adding to the problem.

The south winds growing stronger, fed the fire, carrying the flames north. Merchants on Bennett Avenue, watching as the smoke and flames creep closer just as it had three days earlier, began to panic. This time, freighters had their wagons readily available, charging as much as twenty-five dollars per load to haul the merchant's goods to safety. As the fire approached Bennett Avenue, the firemen again used dynamite to level those buildings in its path, in an effort to halt or at least contain the conflagration. Several buildings were destroyed in rapid succession. This strategy soon backfired. After the firemen placed their powder charges in the building of C. Harder's grocery, they quickly moved the crowd of on-lookers away from the area. At this point, in confusion or lack of communication, a group of volunteer firemen dragged their hoses near the front entrance of the building. Before the hoses were trained on the building, the dynamite exploded. Shattered fragments of glass, burning timber, and mortar flew into the air. The explosion threw many of the volunteers into the street, while the falling debris landing on others, caused severe injuries. A second explosion occurred injured more firemen. George Griffith died at the scene, his head blown off.

The fire moved north, raging for over an hour, engulfing every structure along the alley behind Bennett Avenue, between First and Second streets. The Palace Hotel and Pharmacy, at the southwest corner of Bennett Avenue and Second Street, both went up in flames simultaneously. Miraculously, Sam Altman, owner of the Palace Hotel, had been on the roof of the hotel, pouring water, in an effort to save his establishment. As the heat and smoke intensified, Altman climbed down the outside stairway to safety. Ironically, just two weeks earlier, Altman had received and refused an offer of sixty thousand dollars for the hotel. [12]

By late afternoon, the winds grew stronger, pushing the fire to the north end of town, the predominately residential area. As the fire threatened homes on Carr and Eaton streets, residents were forced to evacuate. Once again, the Sisters of Mercy moved their patients out of the hospital and away to safety. With the residents out of the area, several of the homes were dynamited in an effort to contain the fire. This time it worked. By 4:30 p.m., the Cripple Creek firemen had the fire under control. Tensions were high and tempers flared. As the firemen were leveling the homes with dynamite, one of the residents, Floyd Thompson, witnessed a man deliberately setting fire to a pile of rubbish in an alley. Enraged, Thompson raised his revolver, aimed and shot the man. The body was never claimed and never identified. [13]

The sunrise the following morning was hazy due to smoldering debris all over town. The buildings along the main street of Bennett Avenue were leveled. Residential homes along Carr, Eaton and portions of Golden Avenue, were gone. Only four days after the first fire, Cripple Creek was indeed crippled. Six people died in the fires, several more were injured. Over five thousand citizens were homeless. The value of property lost in the fires was estimated at over two million dollars.

One of the fire fighters, L. M. McBride, later became an explosive engineer. Years after the fires of 1896, McBride wrote:

> "In both fires explosives were used to excess, recklessly, and without concerted action, organization or plan and the use probably assisted the fire as much as it retarded it." [14]

While there is no evidence that Bob Womack was present in the mining district at the time of the fires, he must have been horrified when he did learn of the disaster.

No sooner had the fire been extinguished than rumors of arson began to be whispered through the town. The proprietor of the Portland Hotel had been in lease negotiations with the property owner, Horace Bennett. When the police went to question the hotel manager, they were told that both the proprietor and hotel's chef, Frank Angel, had not been seen since the fire erupted. The police learned that the manager had a dubious background and may have been involved in a series of fires at a hotel he had managed in Ouray. Nothing was ever proven, although the man did lose his position with the hotel. [15]

The *Colorado Springs Gazette*, dated April 30, 1896, delivered the news of the devastating fire under the headline, "Fire at Cripple Creek." The lead article went on to describe the details of the horrible nightmare the citizens of Cripple Creek had suffered. That same day, Cripple Creek city officials received a telegram from Colorado Springs Mayor Hugh Steele, which read:

> "Colorado Springs stands ready to assist your people in every way possible. What can we do?"

Victor's mayor, James Doyle, and the owner of the Portland mine, sent three carloads of blankets, tents, stoves, mattresses and cooking utensils to Cripple Creek aboard the Florence & Cripple Creek Railroad.

In Colorado Springs, Winfield Scott Stratton secured an additional car on the Colorado Midland Terminal Railroad, writing a check for two hundred and fifty dollars. From various Colorado merchants, he received clothing, food and various items which were loaded into the railroad car. The train left Colorado Springs at 6:15 p.m. on April 30, 1896. On board were Verner Z. Reed and Spencer Penrose, representing Stratton's relief team. The train pulled into the charred, but otherwise unscathed brick terminal station at 9 p.m. Reed and Penrose immediately began to survey the devastation. Before the night was over, Reed sent a telegram to Stratton, which was printed in the May 1, 1896, issue of the *Colorado Springs Gazette*:

> "Fire practically under control. No urgent case of want, but our previsions are badly needed. Two killed and several wounded. According to the best information obtainable. Whole business section destroyed. Will wire further information in the morning."

Following the fire, J. M. Roseberry, a wealthy local businessman, financed much of the new construction of Cripple Creek's commercial center. Rather than individual buildings, entire blocks, made of brick were constructed on both sides of Bennett Avenue. On the north side of Bennett Avenue, Charles L. Tutt erected his Tutt Block conveniently between the Cripple Creek Mining Stock Exchange building and the Gold Mining Exchange building. The three-story Gold Mining Stock Exchange went up at the corner of Bennett Avenue and Fourth Street. J. M. Parker rebuilt his First National Bank. By this time, Parker's stockholders were members of the wealthiest of Cripple Creek's citizens and mine owners including Albert E. Carlton, Verner Z. Reed, Winfield Scott Stratton, Spencer Penrose and Charles L. Tutt.

The Fairley brothers were nearly financially ruined when their furniture store was destroyed. In order to recover their business, D. B. and C. W. Fairley took on a partner, Oscar Lampman. Thus, the new partners were able to construct a three-story brick building, stretching the entire block of Third Street at the corner of Bennett Avenue. The building, known as the Fairley & Lampman Block, included the Fairley's furniture store, as well as a variety of businesses, including the first full-service undertaking service in Cripple Creek, offering on-site embalming, coffin sales and funeral and burial services. [15]

Directly north of the Fairley & Lampman Block, Johnny Nolon rebuilt his popular saloon at the same location, the corner of Bennett Avenue and Third Street. Sam Altman rebuilt his Palace Hotel at the same location as the previous hotel, at the corner of Bennett Avenue and Second Street. The three-story brick edifice was known as the Palace Block. Rebuilding also took place north of the commercial district. At the northeast corner of Carr and Third Streets, (a steep sloping corner lot,) just off the main street of Bennett Avenue, J. M. Roseberry built a three-story red brick building which housed the Collins Hotel. [16]

While the citizens of Cripple Creek were rebuilding their town, the mining industry in the Cripple Creek Mining District continued to produce millions in gold ore. Technology was also rapidly providing advancements in the refining process. Charles Tutt and Spencer Penrose had sold their C.O.D mine for three hundred thousand dollars, investing the profits in the future of mining technology. Again, in partnership with W. H. Leonard and Charles MacNeill, Tutt and Penrose established a chlorination mill in the mining camp of Lawrence where their Colorado and Reduction and Refining Company, was located. This proved to be a critical advancement in the treatment of ore processing. In an editorial published in the Cripple Creek's *Evening*

Star newspaper, dated September 18, 1894, the editor wrote:
"Were the old prices in effect, the tonnage of the camp would be very small compared to what it is today."

Although Bob Womack understood very little of this new mining technology, he did know that it was good for the industry and good for the Cripple Creek Mining District. At the age of fifty-two, Bob left his cabin at Poverty Gulch and moved back the Womack family home south of Colorado City. Bob's father, Samuel Redd Womack, now in his seventy-seventh year, was in poor health. His oldest daughter, Eliza, had been caring for him on her own, as well as managing their Sunview Ranch. Now she needed her older brother's help. After much family discussion it was decided that the Sunview Ranch would be sold. With the proceeds from the sale, Eliza would establish a boarding house in Colorado Springs. In this way the elderly Womack patriarch would not only continue to live with his children, but would also be closer to the city's many physicians.

Following the sale of the family ranch, Eliza opened her boarding house at 703 North Cascade Avenue in Colorado Springs. Bob saw to it that his father was comfortably settled into one of the rooms on the main floor, and helped his sister ready the house for boarders. Bob stayed at the boarding house long enough to assure himself that his father was well cared for and his sister's business venture might do very well.

While Eliza may have welcomed her older brother's help, it was not long before she reverted to her old habit of constantly questioning Bob's actions. Bob, frustrated by sister's seemingly endless badgering, once again began spending more and more time at the saloons in Colorado City. However, he quickly became bored and longed for the quiet solitude of his cabin at Poverty Gulch.

Back in the Cripple Creek Mining District, Bob was able to visit with his old friends, ride around the district, see the progress and return for a peaceful night in his cabin at Poverty Gulch. Before winter sent in, Bob would then return to his sister's boarding house in Colorado Springs. Bob continued this routine for the next few years. However, for the entire year of 1898 he stayed in Colorado Springs. That year Bob's brother, William, his wife, Ida, and their daughters, returned to Colorado Springs from Kentucky, where they had lived since returning to their home state in 1885. William Womack quickly found employment as the manager of Antlers Livery Stable. This establishment was located directly across from General William Jackson Palmer's Antlers Hotel, built in 1883 at the west end of Pikes Peak Avenue. When William learned of the impending sale of the Garland Hotel, not far from the Antlers Hotel, he suggested that his sister Eliza purchase the property. Margaret Womack Lowe's husband, Theodore Lowe, now a Denver realtor, arrived in Colorado Springs to facilitate the sale.

Once again, Bob assisted his sister in the new hotel enterprise. He also enjoyed spending time with his brother and nieces. William did his part as well in helping his older sister. William would often steer his customers at the Antlers Livery Stable to the Garland Hotel. Not long after Eliza went into the hotel business, the Antlers Hotel, burned to the ground. Now with only five hotels in town, demand was higher than ever. When investors offered an incredible price for her hotel, Eliza did not hesitate. With the sale of the hotel, Eliza was able to purchase two additional properties located at 121 East Vrain Street and 432 North Nevada Avenue.

In 1902, in preparation for the annual Fourth of July festivities in Cripple Creek, members of the Cripple Creek Elks Club, many of them old friends of Bob's, invited the founder of Cripple Creek, to participate in the event as the Grand Marshal of the parade. Bob was thrilled with the invitation and the chance to spend time with friends again.

Early on the morning of July 3rd, Bob put on his only suit. Not having the need for such attire, Bob had worn the suit at the funeral of his mother and for the wedding reception for his brother William, over twenty years ago. When Bob was finally ready for his trip to Cripple Creek, his brother, William, took him to the depot of the recently established Colorado Springs & Cripple Creek District Railroad.

This new railroad company had been formed by a group of Cripple Creek mine owners, in an effort to compete with the ever-rising freight charges demanded by the Midland Terminal Railroad Company. Included in the group were James Burns, Irving Howbert, William Lennox, J. R. McKinnie, and W. S. Stratton. The forty-five miles of rail lines were built from Colorado Springs, south, passing St. Pete's Dome, and west, climbing to the gold camps of Cameron and Rosemont, nearly a mile above the town of Colorado Springs. From there, two lines were built. One line was constructed south toward the mining town of Victor. The other line was built in a zig-zag formation, over, around and through the mountains. Sixty percent of the rails were built on curves through the mountainous region and over thirty trestles were constructed. Eight tunnels were built by blasting granite walls and fortifying those tunnels with Texas pine. The tunnels were necessary in order to maintain the maximum grade of 3.56%. [17]

Once the rails finally passed through the mountain region, the remainder of the rails were laid westward, passing Womack's Poverty Gulch, with the last rails leading into Cripple Creek. The first train of the Colorado Springs & Cripple Creek District Railroad arrived at the Cripple Creek depot on Warren Avenue, in April 1901. It was the shortest train trip into the district. Thereafter, the S & CCD railroad was forever known as the "Short Line" railroad. [18]

Not long after the inaugural first run of the new railroad, vice president of the United States, Theodore Roosevelt, visited the "The Greatest Gold Camp on Earth," traveling on the Short Line railroad. So impressed with the incredible scenery, Roosevelt famously said, "Bully! This is the ride that bankrupts the English language."

Bob Womack must have had similar thoughts as he gazed out the passenger window at the rocky mountain splendor all around. When the train rolled into the Cripple Creek Mining District, Womack was met at the depot by members of the Elks Club. A member of the Elks Guard then escorted Bob to the Palace Hotel, where his lodging was paid for, courtesy of the Elks Club. The parade began at 10:00 a. m. the following morning. As Grand Marshal, Bob led the parade, riding in a carriage decorated with bouquets of flowers. As the carriage, pulled by six horses, moved slowly down Bennett Avenue, Bob smiled and waved to the crowds lining both sides of the street. The Cripple Creek High School Band followed Bob's carriage.

By all accounts the Fourth of July celebration of 1902 was a fine affair. One of those accounts appeared in July 5, 1902, issue of the *Colorado Springs Gazette* newspaper. The article, under the headline, "Big Celebration Was An Unqualified Success - Big Crowds Were Out," the article read in part:

> "The people of the gold camp and thousands of visitors from outside points celebrated the Fourth of July in an appropriate and noisy manner in Cripple Creek. The parade formed promptly at 10:30 a.m. Then came a six-horse, gaily decorated carriage, in which was seated Bob Womack, the father of the Cripple Creek district. All along the line of march the old prospector was cheered."

The article went on to recount the day's events, but ended with this:

> "Fourth of July accidents were not numerous here today, but two boys who fooled with the dangerous cannon cracker

were compelled to call upon physicians to attend their injuries. Clifford Loud, aged 15 years, the son of Mr. and Mrs, B. Loud, lost two fingers and a thumb on his right hand by the explosion of a cannon cracker. R. T. Jamison, aged thirteen years, who lives with his parents on El Paso Avenue, lost a finger. Dr. Hereford attended the injuries."

After the parade, everyone gathered for the traditional hard-rock drilling contest. It was during this event, that Bob was finally able to visit with old friends. Sadly, the group was growing smaller. Many of the millionaire miners had moved to Colorado Springs, men like Stratton, Penrose and Tutt. One of Bob's oldest friends, Levi Welty was dead, as was his son, George Welty. Alonzo Welty and his wife died in a horrific carriage accident. Sam Strong, whom Bob had helped locate a mining claim back in the early days of 1892, was dead. The previous year, Strong had been murdered in the Newport Saloon, located in the Mining Exchange Building, by the saloon owner, J. Grant Crumley.

It just so happened that Hiram Rogers, the *Colorado Springs Gazette* reporter who had written about Bob Womack for years, usually in an unfavorable light, was in Cripple Creek to cover the Fourth of July events. On the return train trip to Colorado Springs, Rogers spoke to Womack. When asked about the changes in Cripple Creek, Bob Womack remarked:

"This is one fine city, this Cripple Creek."

Soon after Bob's trip to Cripple Creek, he learned that one of his oldest friends, Winfield Scott Stratton, was gravely ill. Bob had helped Stratton locate his rich Independence mine, which had made Stratton Cripple Creek's first millionaire. Over the next several years, the Independence mine not only added millions to Stratton's bank account, the mine also provided hundreds of jobs in the Cripple Creek Mining District.

On April 18, 1900, Stratton had sold the Independence mine for ten million dollars, the highest price for any Cripple Creek mine. [19] Despite Stratton's millionaire status, he remained loyal to his friends, including Bob Womack. Over the years, Stratton had often given Bob money when he was down on his luck. Now, it was Bob's turn to return the favor, as best he could. Bob often visited his old friend at his home on Weber Street, in Colorado Springs. As the months went by, Stratton's illness, later determined as cirrhosis of the liver, worsened. On the morning of Saturday, September 13, 1902, Winfield Scott Stratton slipped into a coma. That night, at 9:35 p.m., Stratton died. [20]

On Tuesday, September 16, 1902, Stratton's funeral was held. Bob Womack attended the solemn service, once again dressed in his only black suit. The following day Stratton's body was was buried in a somewhat secluded plot, surrounded by trees and shrubs, at Colorado Spring's Evergreen Cemetery. [21]

Following the labor strike of 1894, the Western Federation of Miners, under the leadership of Edward Boyce, had become the strongest industrial labor union in the country. With their headquarters in Denver, the WFM also became a powerful political force in Colorado. The leader of this movement inside the WFM organization was William "Big Bill" Haywood. With the death of Winfield Scott Stratton, the Cripple Creek Mining District's wealthiest and most powerful mine owner, officials of the WFM saw their opportunity to force a strike and gain power in the district. It was under Haywood's direction that nearly four thousand union members were ordered to strike. It was a perfect set-up for a labor war.

As a child, Leslie Doyle Spell had watched Bob Womack and others work their claims. By 1903 twenty-one year old Spell had realized his own dream of becoming a miner. Unfortunately, Spell, found himself caught in middle of the labor strike of 1903-1904. Spell later described the events leading up to the strike:

"This strike was called in behalf of the men working in the
smelters, who were poorly paid for their long hours. Both miners
and smelter men were union organizations, so for the benefit
of the smelter men we miners felt we should protect them by
refusing to produce and ship to the smelter plants who were
employed by non-union men. The sad condition then was that
union smelter men came to the mines and took jobs rightfully
belonging to miners, as the pay was better. Before the close of
every union meeting a short pledge was given the men by the
officer that all strikers would be law-abiding citizens and refrain
from any violence. In some cases it appeared to me as though
the militia was at the bottom of our troubles and seemed to
incite disturbances. We tried peaceable methods, trying to play
a neutral part with both sides, but discovered when one rode the
fence, he becomes a target for both sides. We were able to keep
out of serious trouble until June of 1904." [22]

The powerful Western Federation of Miners had successfully organized
their miners to strike in mining areas across Colorado. Governor James
H. Peabody had pledged to stop the strikes and began reorganizing the
Colorado National Guard for that purpose. Peabody appointed Sherman
M. Bell, a Cripple Creek mine manager, as his adjutant general. Next,
Peabody ordered the Colorado State Militia to be on standby pending
his orders. [23]

When Denver journalists learned of the governor's plans, Peabody
was mocked and ridiculed in political cartoons. Under such criticism
Governor Peabody backed down. One leader who did not back down
was Colorado's Catholic Bishop, Nicholas C. Matz. In his appearances
in Denver and across the state, Matz often decried that the forced strikes
of the WFM were evil and akin to socialism. Again, the Denver papers

seemed to ridicule those who took a position against the labor union. The *Rocky Mountain News*, in their coverage of the Bishop's various speeches, chose the following quote to include in their article:

"Socialism will burn the souls of such reckless leaders of the Western Federation of Miners for all eternity in hell."

What Denver journalists failed to understand was that thousands of miners were out of work due to the on-going strike. While it is hard to imagine that Governor Peabody did not realize the enormous effect of the unemployment across the state, he hesitated to take any action. Then, on September 4, 1904, Governor Peabody sent one thousand soldiers, under Adjutant General Sherman M. Bell, to the Cripple Creek Mining District. Leslie Doyle Spell described the horrific events that followed:

"At Anaconda, in the Cripple Creek Mining District, we arose one morning to find the town in turmoil. In fact, the whole district was in an uproar over trouble that had happened early in the morning. A bomb had been placed under the platform of the railroad station at Independence where strike-breaking miners were accustomed to board the train at two o'clock in the morning after finishing the night shift. It exploded with a terrific din, blowing platform and men to bits. Thirteen men were killed and many more horribly wounded. What had been a peaceful early morning scene with a group of tired men became a tangled, gory mass of wreckage. Bodies were horribly mangled and the early morning air filled with cries and moans of the wounded."

The bloodshed continued. Harry Orchard, a union member of the WFM, had been employed at the Vindicator mine. As the labor strike wore on, Orchard had been hoarding large amounts of high grade ore inside the closed mine. One day, Orchard took several sticks of dynamite into the mine. Once he had placed them at the sixth level of the mine, Orchard rigged the dynamite with a loaded pistol, to the mine's cage shaft. In this way, when someone took the cage down the shaft of the mine, the cage would hit the trigger, causing the dynamite to explode. Harry Orchard's scheme eventually caused the damage and death he intended. Melvin Beck and Charles McCormick, both supervisors of the Vindicator mine, took the cage down the shaft to the sixth level of the mine. As the cage stopped, Orchard's rigged pistol went off. The dynamite exploded, instantly killing both Beck and Charles McCormick. The shaft caved in, rendering the Vindicator mine inoperable.

Orchard wasn't finished. Next, he rigged dynamite to explode at the train depot at the Independence mine. At the mine's shift change, 2 a.m., on June 6, 1904, twenty three miners were gathered at the depot awaiting the train from Victor. Fifteen minutes later, as the train approached and the whistle blew, an explosion rocked the depot. Men were thrown from the platformhen another explosion ripped into half of the building sending debris through the air. Thirteen men lost their lives and several others were maimed for live.

Mine owners were aghast at the murderous turn the labor strike had taken. Citizens of the Cripple Creek Mining District were outraged. It was not long before leaders of the Citizen's Alliance and the Mine Owners Association, converged in the mining district of Cripple Creek. Clarence Hamlin, secretary of the Citizen's Alliance, wasted no time in scheduling a mass meeting, held on the streets of Victor. Leslie Doyle Spell not only witnessed the occasion, but became a victim of the violence that quickly erupted. Spell wrote his account years later:

"Knowing that no help could be expected from the militia, these men turned to the sheriff, a man named Robertson. He felt as we did, neutral and attempting to help both sides. The governor, as yet had not had time to declare martial law, even though the militia was still stationed near Goldfield. The larger part of the crowd had gone to Victor, about three miles from the scene of the explosion. I had to pass through Victor on my way home, but filled with curiosity, stopped there to see what was happening. My last thought was that I would get into trouble of any kind. On Fourth Street was the Union Hall, a brick building with plastered interior, offices, and tall windows on the second floor. About fifty of the men, including myself, had climbed the stairs and gone into the front offices, posting ourselves at the front windows where we could look down over the crowd assembled below. Hamlin, secretary of the Citizen's Alliance, was speaking in such a manner as to incite the crowd's anger against the union men. 'Run 'em all out, all their lice and nits too.' The crowd seethed with excitement. Alf Miller, a striker over six feet and weighing about two hundred pounds, had taken on a bit too much liquor and struck a man with a blow, which precipitated a free-for-all fist fight. A man directly in back of Alf picked up a rock the size of a dinner plate, raised it ready to bring it down on his head, when a shot rang out and the man with the rock slumped to the ground with a bullet through his heart. This was followed by a flurry of shots and the crowd dispersed as rapidly as possible. It seemed to us, watching from the windows above, a miracle more weren't killed or wounded from the number of guns firing. Sitting in the front window as I was, I had a clear vision of the entire proceedings and I can truthfully say that never a shot was fired from the windows of the hall. The militia, from where it was quartered, heard the shooting and rushed to the scene of the riot. The soldiers immediately stationed themselves on the adjacent buildings which were on a higher level, thus affording an excellent opportunity to shoot down into the windows of our building. By then I realized I had blundered into a most unfortunate predicament from which there was no escape.

It seemed to me the plaster of the walls moved in on us from the hail of bullets of the soldiers. Every window in the building was smashed and the front wall riddled with bullets. We all rushed to the center of the building, for shots from the militia stationed on the higher buildings were ranging downwards, with bullets from the men in the streets ranging upwards. Thus we were cut in a crossfire, but strangely enough, only four of our men were wounded or killed.

McManus, one of our men, quick of thought and with iron nerve, rushed to a side window facing the soldiers and waved his handkerchief shouting: 'Stop, stop shooting. We surrender.' Another of our men had been hit by a bullet from a Craig-Jorgenson rifle used by the militia. The bullet had passed through the wall, hitting him. He fell to the floor and screamed: 'I'm shot, I'm shot, I'm killed.'

By this time the mob on the street was rushing into the building and up the stairs. We were ordered to hold up our hands. We were searched three or four times, shoved around, kicked, beaten, and cursed and threatened with our lives if we so much as batted an eye. Some of our men were badly mauled during this melee and one almost scalped with a bayonet. Outside on the street we were lined up in single file, I being the first in line, then marched with our hands up in the air, guns pointing at our heads from every angle. The captain of the company walked backwards with his gun nudged against my stomach, cursing and saying: 'It you make a crooked move, I'll blow your guts out.' I was scared within an inch of my life. More than fifty years have passed since that experience, but I can truthfully say that it was the most terrifying one for me." [24]

The following morning, Adjutant General Sherman M. Bell, arrived in the mining district. Within a matter of days, Bell and his soldiers were able to restore order in the region. Bell then rounded up some two hundred members of the Western Federation of Miners. The men were escorted by armed guards to the Midland Terminal depot. Once aboard the train, the union men were transported to approximately two hundred miles east to the state's border with Kansas. From there, the men were taken off the train and forced to walk across the state line. In the end, the violent actions of the union labor strike undercut union solidarity and drove the WFM out of the Cripple Creek Mining District.

Bob Womack was horrified by the murderous events in the mining district that he had created back in 1891. Not long after the strike ended, Bob decided to make one more trip to his beloved region of Cripple Creek. Once again, Bob took the Short Line Railroad into the mining district, arriving on July 28, 1904. Bob spent a few days roaming the area, and visiting with old friends.

Before he left the district, Bob spent some quiet time at his old cabin in Poverty Gulch. Perhaps he was reflecting on days gone by, of the eighteen-year search for the illusive gold vein which he finally located, creating the greatest gold rush in Colorado's history. Or Bob may have been remembering better days with his old friends, most of whom were now deceased. In any case, he definitely enjoyed being away from his nagging sister, Eliza.

Finally, Bob left Poverty Gulch and made his way to the train depot on Warren Avenue. As he boarded the Florence & Cripple Creek train, Bob Womack had no idea he was leaving his beloved Cripple Creek for the last time.

Once again, Bob chose to sit by the window, where he could gaze at the majestic scenery as the train rolled through, around and over the mountains. At the train station in Colorado Springs, Bob was happy to see his brother, William, and his youngest niece, Dorsey, there to greet him. Since William and his family had returned to Colorado Springs, Bob and his youngest niece had become very close. Evidently, the cool mountain air on the train trip proved too much for the ailing prospector. Bob developed what he thought was a common cold. As his condition grew worse, Bob lost the use of his left arm. A doctor diagnosed Bob's condition as partial paralysis. In a short amount of time, Bob's entire left side was paralyzed.

While Eliza still ran her boarding house on Nevada Avenue, she had long since closed the business on East Vrain Street. Now, with Bob's paralyzed condition, Eliza set up a room on the main floor for her brother. Eliza's impatience with her older brother seemed to quickly fade away. Whether Bob was aware of the change in his sister's demeanor or not, he was extremely grateful for her help. William and his daughters often visited Bob and Sam at Eliza's house. However, William's youngest daughter, Dorsey, visited her favorite uncle every day. Although Bob was bedridden, he was able to play cards and board games with Dorsey. But he enjoyed most was their long conversations, or when Dorsey would read to him. Fifteen year old Dorsey Womack was a very resourceful young lady. Somehow Dorsey had managed a meeting with the editor of the *Colorado Springs Gazette* newspaper, Charles T. Wilder. During this meeting, Dorsey explained the debilitating condition of her Uncle Bob, reminding the editor that it was Bob Womack who first discovered gold in the Cripple Creek Mining District.

After the meeting, Wilder took the information Dorsey had provided to his employer, Clarence P. Dodge, owner of the publication. After much discussion, the two newspapermen started a relief fund for Bob Womack. Wilder announced the effort in the February 9, 1908, issue of the *Colorado Springs Gazette*. Under the headline, "A Relief Fund For Bob Womack," the editor asked for the public's contributions of fifty dollars to the cause. The accompanying article followed the headline announcement.

"Bob Womack Is A Helpless Paralytic Entirely Dependent On Care Of Faithful Sister Discoverer of Cripple Creek whose gold fields have yielded nearly a quarter of a billion dollars in the last 25 years, 'Bob' Womack is today a helpless invalid, wholly dependent for his support upon a loving sister. To ease the pathway of his declining years and to provide means for treatment whereby he may be able to recover the use of his limbs, now numbed by paralysis, the Gazette today issues a general appeal to the people of Colorado Springs to subscribe to a relief fund. Since the publication of an editorial in the Gazette last Wednesday referring to the great future of of the Cripple Creek district and to the tremendous benefits 'Bob' Womack conferred through his discovery in the winter of 1891, many letters and expressions of sympathy have been received, and it has been this fact, together with the unquestioned merits of the case that has led the Gazette to undertake this movement. Womack was struck with paralysis three years ago, and since that time has been helpless. From that day to this, with the exception of three months when he was in Pueblo, taking mineral water baths, he has lain in bed, unable to move his left side. The ministrations of his sister, Miss Eliza G. Womack, are all that have kept 'Bob' Womack and his father, who is now his 94th year, alive. For a long time Miss Womack conducted a boarding house, but of late, her other work has been such a tax upon her strength that she has been obliged to give up the business, and the income from that source has ceased, adding to the burden. It is thought by Mr. Womack that under the care of specialists he could regain the use of his arm and limbs. Thus, the purpose and object of this subscription fund." [25]

The following week, the *Colorado Springs Gazette* ran an article recounting Bob's historic gold find, the local mining industry that followed, and the thousands of jobs created in the region. The article appeared in the February 16, 1908, issue of the *Colorado Springs Gazette*. The headline read, "Discoverer of Cripple Creek Penniless." The short article followed:

> "Bob Womack, whose pick unloosed a quarter of a billion dollar flow of gold, is a helpless paralytic. His golden El Dorado poured a glittering stream of wealth into the world, creating luxury, ease and happiness. Robert Womack, 'the father of Cripple Creek,' discoverer of the 'greatest gold camp' in the world's history, is helpless and penniless. There are few visitors at his unpretentious cottage at 419 North Nevada Avenue, as few who care to relieve the tedium of an invalid's exile. But there, tossing feverishly under the restraint of his affliction, Robert Womack prays for the day when he shall be made whole, when again he can shoulder a miner's pick and discover a new Cripple Creek."

However, by the end of that summer, Wilder, the editor of the *Colorado Springs Gazette*, had received less then a thousand dollars toward his goal of five thousand dollars. In the August 31, 1908, issue of the paper, Wilder suspended the fund raising effort for Bob Womack. The following day, the paper printed a letter to the editor, under the headline, "Relief Fund For Bob Womack."

> "To the editor of the Gazette,
>
> Noticing the short article in Wednesday's Gazette halting the fund. Speaking for Cripple Creek and 'Bob' Womack as the

father of the most famous gold mining camp in the world, we feel impelled to state a few facts in regard to his present condition. We believe that most of our citizens know that 'Bob' Womack discovered what is now known as the 'Gold King' mining property, the first mine discovered in the famous Cripple Creek district. Two years ago 'Bob' Womack was stricken with paralysis and has been an absolutely helpless invalid ever since, cared for by his sister. It now seems to be a case of 'What is everyone's business is no one's business.' Sincerely hoping that the many citizens of Colorado Springs who have derived all the comforts and luxuries of life from 'Bob' Womack's discovery of Cripple Creek will come to aid of the sick man."

Charles T. Wilder turned the collected money over to Eliza Womack. Eliza and William admitted Bob to the Glockner Hospital, where the money was used to pay for new treatments for Bob's paralysis. Within a few months, the doctors began to see some improvement in Bob's condition. Bob's favorite niece, Dorsey, came to hospital every day. The two continued with their old routine, playing card games, and having long conversations. Dorsey also read the *Colorado Springs Gazette* newspaper articles to him. It was from these readings that Bob learned of the death of his long-time friend, Charles L. Tutt, who had died on January 21, 1909. Then, just two months later, Dorsey read to her uncle the many accounts of the death of General William Jackson Palmer on March 13, 1909.

The *Colorado Springs Gazette* ran a full page article in the July 31, 1909, issue of the paper. Under the headline, "Holding His Own And May Now Pull Through," a photograph of Bob Womack was included with article which read in part:

"Bob Womack, the veteran prospector who first discovered gold at Cripple Creek, still has a fair chance for recovery. He has not grown worse during the past week and last night word from the Glockner, where he is cared for, was to the effect that he was holding his own, having had no change whatever during the day. His physician holds out hope for his recovery but the old man has weathered so many storms that his system is not what it used to be and it largely depends on his vitality as to whether he gets out of bed again."

It was also in July 1909 that Dorsey Womack and a group of friends took a trip to Pueblo, Colorado. During the excursion, Dorsey fell ill. Thinking it was just a cold or possibly the flu, Dorsey remained in Pueblo with her friends. A few days later, Dorsey fainted. Unable to revive her, Dorsey's friends frantically searched for a doctor. Eventually, Dorsey was taken to a local hospital. William Womack caught the next train and rushed to his daughter's bedside. It is not known if Dorsey ever regained consciousness. A week later, sixteen year old Dorsey Womack died. It was later revealed the young teenager died of typhoid fever. [26]

Eliza broke the news of Dorsey's death to Bob, who was obviously shocked. Not only was Bob devastated by the death of his beloved niece, he was simply helpless to be of any comfort to his family. Meanwhile, William Womack brought his youngest daughter's body back to Colorado Springs for burial. Following the funeral, Dorsey Womack was buried in the family plot at the Evergreen Cemetery in Colorado Springs. The second burial in the Womack family plot, Dorsey was laid not far from her grandmother, Corella Booker Womack's gravesite. [27]

Not long after the death of Dorsey, the money from Bob's relief fund ran out. Eliza and William brought Bob back to Eliza's home on Nevada Street. Eliza's difficulties in caring for both her father and her brother, not to mention the financial strain, became overwhelming. Margaret Womack soon came to aid of her younger sister.

Following the death of her first husband, Theodore Lowe, Margaret had married Jack Edwards, an executive with the Singer Sewing Machine Company. Edwards had received an assignment in New Mexico, which would keep him away for an extended period of time. Because Margaret would be accompanying her husband on the trip, she offered her home to Eliza. Thus, Eliza was able to reopen her home to boarders for the needed income, while her father and brother were cared for in a private residence.

After Dorsey's death Bob became despondent. Thus, his health suffered. Not a week had passed after Bob and his father were moved into Margaret's home that Bob slipped into a coma. Eliza summoned several doctors, but all agreed there was nothing to be done and the end was near. A week later, at approximately 6;30 a.m., on August 10, 1909, with his father and sister at his bedside, Robert Miller Womack died. He was sixty-six years old.

The *Colorado Springs Gazette* printed the obituary in the August 11, 1909, issue:

"Discoverer of Great Gold Camp Dies Penniless 'Bob' Womack, the Father of Cripple Creek, Succumbs to Paralysis Grief Hastens Death Dug First Shaft in District, Destined to Yield Hundreds of Millions of Dollars Robert M. Womack, discoverer of Cripple Creek, which has since produced upwards of $250,000,000 in gold, died penniless at his home, 117 South Limit street, yesterday morning, after lying, a helpless paralytic, for nearly six years. Womack's death was hastened by the death of his niece, Dorsey Womack, 16 years old, which occurred two weeks ago. The child had been a great favorite with him, and her loss took from him the strength with which he had fought, ever hoping for the time when he might again take up the quest of gold and, profiting by it, perhaps gain new fortunes. Womack's death occurred peacefully at 6 o'clock yesterday morning. It had been expected, since for the last few days he had gradually grown weaker, despite the tender mercies of his sister. Womack was 66 years of age and unmarried, and is survived also by a sister Elizabeth, and brother, W. W. Womack, living at 736 West Huerfano street. The death of Womack, marks the passing of the fourth pioneer in this city within a week. Last Monday John Wolfe died at the age of 79, and yesterday morning, almost at the same time of Womack's death, A. J. Bayne, aged 72, passed away. Last Friday Mrs. Anthony Bolt, a pioneer of Colorado City, died at her home there. 'Bob' Womack, as he had been known for the past two decades to all who knew him, was born in Kentucky, where the family lived on a farm until he was 12 years old. Then they started west and settled near Fountain, 13 miles south of this city, where the elder Womack bought a ranch. In the early days he moved farther into the mountains, buying the Welty property, which occupied the present site of Cripple Creek, little dreaming that his son, herding their cattle on the green slopes, where in the dead of winter the snow seldom lay for a day, would be the discoverer of a mining camp which would come to be known as one of the greatest on the globe. The father, now past 95 years of age, is still living and hearty. The funeral service will be conducted from the undertaking rooms of Fairley & Law at 3 o'clock this afternoon, and interment, which will be private, will be in Evergreen cemetery."

On the afternoon of August 11, 1909, Robert "Bob" Miller Womack, was laid to rest in the Womack family plot at Evergreen Cemetery in Colorado Springs. His grave site lay next to that of his beloved niece, Dorsey, and very near his mother, Corella. [28]

The following day, the *Colorado Springs Gazette* printed the details of the funeral service in an article dated August 12, 1909.

"Bob Womack Laid To Rest Yesterday Flags in Camp He Discovered at Halfmast During the Funeral Service The funeral of 'Bob' Womack, the discoverer of Cripple Creek, was held from the undertaking rooms of Fairley & Law yesterday afternoon at 3 o'clock. The Rev. G. B. Stewart conducted the services, which were attended by a large number of Mr. Womack's friends and pioneer residents of the country. The pallbearers were Frank Cotten, James Barnes, B. G. Robbins, John Keyes, B. L. Evans and John Sitlington. Interment, which was at Evergreen cemetery, was private. During the hour of the service flags on public and private buildings in the Cripple Creek district were placed at halfmast in respect to the memory of the camp's discoverer."

Two days later, on August 14, 1904, the *Colorado Springs Gazette* printed a fine tribute to Bob Womack:

Among the clouds we looped the loop
Far on to Cripple Creek
We saw the sun change to gold
The eight-mile distant peak
We saw the lifted shaft house
Upon a far-off height
And turned our eyes obedient
As guides called 'left' or 'right'
From mountain top to mountain top
The mines showed picturesque
With smokestacks high and piles of earth gray, grim, sometimes grotesque
Each pointed to piles of gray-green drift
Mimicked a mountain peak
An Aladdin land of wonders
Seemed the caves of Cripple Creek.

The mining camp of Elkton was home to several rich gold mines. (Denver Public Library, Western History Department, X-8178)

Governor Davis Waite's militia were deployed to stop the labor strike. (Denver Public Library, Western History Department, P-1999)

The militia set up a tent camp in a valley below Battle Mountain. (Denver Public Library, Western History Department, X-60253

State troops attempt to keep peace during the labor riot. (Denver Public Library, Western History Department, X-60327)

Cripple Creek was a bustling town by 1896. It was also a tinderbox. (Denver Public Library, Western History Department, X-798)

In April 1896 fire exploded and raged through Cripple Creek. (Denver Public Library, Western History Department, X-869)

Panic set in as townsfolk watched buildings burn. (Denver Public Library, Western History Department, X-868)

Cripple Creek lays in smoldering ruins in the early morning sunlight after the fire. (Denver Public Library, Western History Department, P-812)

Cripple Creek quickly rebuilt after the fires, bigger and better than ever, despite the unevenness of Bennett Avenue. (Denver Public Library, Western History Department, X-21362)

Bob Womack traveled to Cripple Creek on the Colorado Springs and Cripple Creek District Railroad. Locomotive #8 arrives in Cripple Creek. (Denver Public Library, Western History Department, Z-5336)

Named after Colorado Senator Henry M. Teller, Teller County was created in 1900. (Denver Public Library, Western History Department, F-10085)

Cripple Creek prided themselves on the town parades like this one in 1896.
(Denver Public Library, Western History Department, X-607)

William G. "Big Bill" Haywood organized the Western Federation of Miners to strike in 1903-1904. (Denver Public Library, Western History Department, Bio-FF)

The state militia raise the flag during the labor wars of 1903-1904, something Leslie Spell must have witnessed. (Denver Public Library, Western History Department, X-60321)

Following the labor strike the mines in the District returned to normal ore production levels. (Denver Public Library, Western History Department, X-63217)

In 1902, Bob Womack was the Grand Marshal in the Fourth of July parade in Cripple Creek. Womack would die seven years later. (Author's Collection, gift from Dr. Tom Noel.)

Robert Miller "Bob" Womack was buried in the Womack family plot in Evergreen Cemetery in Colorado Springs. (Author's Collection)

Epilogue

Samuel Redd Womack outlived his oldest son, Robert Miller, by nearly ten years. Six months before his death, the ninety-nine year old patriarch of the family gave an interview to a reporter with the *Colorado Springs Gazette*. The piece, with a few exaggerations, ran in the Sunday, January 12, 1919, issue of the paper:

> "Samuel Redd Womack, in 11 months will have reached his hundredth birthday. He discovered the first silver mine in Colorado, near Georgetown, and his son, Robert Womack, who died several years ago at the age of 66, not to be outdone, discovered the first gold mine at what is now Cripple Creek. From the windows of his house, with vision that has grown dim, Mr. Womack now watches people passing to and fro on the sidewalk. His daughter, Miss E. G. Womack, reads him the newspapers and keeps him informed. The once man of affairs in the state, he has become a mere spectator in life. 'How does it feel to live a hundred years?'
> Womack—'Oh, I don't want to feel it a second time - after all

that I have been through, it seems a very long time, as I look back. Its too long to take in. My mind is beginning to fail me. I was born near Lexington, Kentucky and came to Colorado. I went to Idaho Springs and later, bringing my family, which consisted of my wife, my sons and one daughter. I was convinced from all I heard that there must be gold at Pikes Peak. I sent my sons there to search for it. They went through the region, too and fro. They found several indications of gold, [but] they could not find the vein, which in those days was all that anybody thought worth the trouble. I cannot remember just when it was that I came to live in this part of the state. I owned and controlled, according to the custom of the day, a very large tract of land and raised cattle on it. My son, Robert, worked with me, but he kept talking of gold at what is now Cripple Creek, and finally one winter, when there was not much work to do at the ranch, he went up there and searched until he found gold. I had myself discovered the first silver mine in the state, the Seaton mine, near Georgetown. Yes, I can look back a long way and recall many things. I was in the south [sic] during the Civil War, but I could never be called a southerner, for I was opposed to the war. I did not think from the first that it would be the best thing for the south. My wife died in 1887, but I have one of the best daughters who ever lived. She has stayed with me and taken care of me, so I have not been alone, by any means.'

Mr. Womack has a son, William W. Womack, who lives at 121 East St. Vrain street."

Indeed, it seems as if Sam Womack's mind may have become a bit cloudy with the fog of age. Sam's wife, Corella Booker Womack, died in 1879, not in 1887. Further, while there were many silver claims filed in Clear Creek County, during Sam Womack's time there, the Seaton claim, on Seaton Mountain was not the first. According to the "History of Clear Creek and Gilpin Counties," that honor is attributed to the Johnson Lode on Burrell Hill, near Georgetown.

Nevertheless, Sam did not live to reach his one hundredth birthday. Samuel Redd Womack died peacefully on June 8, 1919, just three months shy of that birthday landmark. The *Colorado Springs Gazette* printed the obituary in the June 9, 1919, issue:

> "Samuel R. Womack, who came here before there was any Colorado Springs and watched the city build up around him, died yesterday at his home, at the age of 99 years and seven months. He was the father of Robert Womack, discoverer of the first gold mine at Cripple Creek. At one time he owned large tracts of land where the city now stands. For a number of years he has been too feeble to leave his house, and was nearly blind. The funeral will be held at 3 o'clock this afternoon at the Fairley undertaking rooms. The Rev. Claire E. Waite will officiate. Burial will be in Evergreen cemetery. Mrs. Womack died years ago."

A small funeral was held, with burial following. The patriarch of the Womack family was buried in the family plot next to his wife, Corella.

As the years went on, Eliza continued with her boarding house business. Evidently William, and his wife, Ida, may have been struggling a bit financially, as the above article from the *Colorado Springs Gazette*, notes William's address as that of Eliza's boarding house.

On Saturday, December 17, 1927, Elizabeth G. Womack died in her home. The *Colorado Springs Gazette* printed the obituary in the Sunday, December 18, 1927, issue of the paper, which read in part:

> "Sister of Founder of Cripple Creek Dies at Home Here Will

Hold Services For Miss Eliza Womack on Monday Afternoon
Miss Eliza Womack, sister of Robert Womack, discoverer of
gold in Cripple Creek, died yesterday morning at her home,
121 East St. Vrain street. She was 79 years of age. She leaves a
brother, W. W. Womack of this city. The funeral will be held at
2 o'clock tomorrow afternoon at the Law chapel. Burial will be
in Evergreen cemetery."

Elizabeth G. Womack's obituary, while printed on the front page
of the paper, only contained this small bit of information about the
deceased woman. However, the two-column piece went on to extol the
history of her brother, Robert "Bob" Miller Womack, which was carried
on to pages five and six of the newspaper.

Following the death of Eliza, William and his wife, Ida, continued to
live at the home on East St. Vrain Street. It was there, that on the morning
of April 19, 1931, William W. Womack died, at the age of eighty. The
Colorado Springs Gazette printed the obituary in a column on the front
page of the April 20, 1931, issue:

"William Womack, Region Pioneer Dies At Home Family
Famous for First Discovery of Gold at Cripple Creek.
William Womack, whose name is closely linked with mining
and livestock history of the Pikes peak [sic] region, died yesterday
morning at his home, 121 East St. Vrain street. On June 24 this
year he would have been 81 years old. He was ill only a short
time. Mr. Womack's residency here began in 1861. There was
no Colorado Springs when, at the age of 16, he first passed
the foot of Pikes peak. Civil war was brewing when Samuel
Womack, father of William, decided to move with his family
from Kentucky to Colorado. Arriving in this state in April
1861, the family settled at Idaho Springs. Prospecting in the hills

west of Denver, the elder Womack discovered a silver deposit, a 'strike' which became the Seaton mine, one of the most famous in the mining annuals of Colorado. Samuel Womack and his family came to this region and for two years the elder Womack searched the sides of Pikes peak for silver deposits, after which he engaged in ranching on Little Fountain creek. Ranching eventually led the Womack boys, William and Robert, into the Cripple Creek district in their search for desirable grazing land. There they obtained possession of land by purchasing the Welty brothers' squatter's rights for $500 in cash. This piece of land is situated within a short distance of the place where Robert Womack made his gold find that brought the Cripple Creek rush of 1892. Securing water rights, within a short time they had an area of land six square miles, fenced and where Cripple Creek now stands roamed the Womack herd of 1,000 purebred Shorthorn cattle. Riding on horseback over the homestead one day in 1888, William came across a piece of rock that appeared to contain gold, He sent the rock to Denver where it assayed $100 worth of gold to the ton. He had the tract surveyed and began prospecting, but found nothing of material value. Ill health a little later forced him to leave the Cripple Creek district and he went back to Kentucky for four years. Robert, meanwhile, continued to prospect now and then and one day opened a vein of gold which subsequently became known as the Gold King vein, a rich strike made 40 feet up the slope from the place where William had found his rich piece of gold ore. With the discovery of the Gold King vein the Cripple Creek rush got under way. On returning to Colorado Springs from Kentucky, William Womack operated the Antlers livery on Cascade Avenue. His brother, Robert, died in 1911 and father in 1919. William Womack is survived by his wife, Ida V. Womack, four daughters, Mrs. J. E. Edwards, Denver, Mrs. Homer Davis, Mrs. I. O. Wasson and Mrs. Alex Fluk of Colorado Springs, six grandchildren and one great grandchild."

There are several interesting points in this obituary regarding the history of William W. Womack. First, there is no evidence that William found a "rich piece of gold ore." If he had, the next logical step would have been to file a mining claim, particularly if the ore sample assayed at such a high value as claimed in the piece. There is no such recording in the El Paso County records. Second, Robert "Bob' Womack died in August 1909, not 1911. The third point is perhaps the most revealing. The reason given for William Womack's return to Kentucky was given as "ill health." This suggests that William's widow, Ida, provided the information to the writer for the *Colorado Springs Gazette*. Ever since William brought his bride, the former Ida Van Dyck, to Sunview Ranch, the Womack family ranch, their was tension within the family. Bob did not care for his new sister-in-law, and Eliza had constant heated arguments with Ida. This eventually led to the true reason William and Ida returned to Kentucky. Perhaps Ida, bitter that she was never accepted into the Womack family, slanted the version of events.

A final interesting point is that in the obituary, there is no mention of a funeral service or burial ceremony. William W. Womack was buried in a small plot, not far from the entrance of the Evergreen Cemetery. It was purposely purchased by Ida V. Womack, and lay at the opposite end of the cemetery from the Womack family plot. This, despite the fact that her daughter Dorsey's grave lay in the original Womack family plot.

William Womack's widow, Ida V. Womack, seemed to harbor bitter feelings toward her in-laws. In the January 23, 1938, seven years after the death of her husband, Ida Womack gave an in-depth interview to C. B. Dudley, a reporter for the *Colorado Springs Gazette*. Under the headline, "Last of the Womacks of Cripple Creek Fame Plans To Go Back This Spring Despite Earlier Vows," Ida's account of historic events understandably seem sentimental, yet also smacked of her disdain for the Womack family, and Bob Womack in particular.

"Mrs. Ida V. Womack, widow of William W. Womack, whom she considers the discoverer of gold in Cripple Creek, rather than his brother, Bob Womack, as generally believed, may go to Cripple Creek. Altho [sic] she is a pioneer resident of Colorado Springs, and in the late 1880s picked wild raspberries where some of the most famous mines of the district are, she has never seen the town of Cripple Creek. She is the last of the Womack family, which had in their grasp the greatest gold deposits the United States has ever known, and let them slip thru [sic] their fingers. So chagrined was she by the loss that she determined never again to go near the place. And she has kept her vow. But now her granddaughter, Mrs. Loren Chamberlain of Cripple Creek, is urging her after all, to return to the district. And Mrs. Womack who is 83 years old and lives at 121 East St. Vrain street, is beginning to weaken in her self-imposed exile. 'On some pleasant day when spring comes,' she said last week, 'I may go up to Cripple Creek. I don't know whether the log cabin in which I lived when my husband had the only mine there is still standing. Some say it is, and say it isn't. I would like to go and see. There was a meadow in which there seemed to be a rising and sinking effect - I don't know why - and the mountains were west of the cabin. Tho the altitude was high I did not mind it, but rode horseback and picked the most wonderful raspberries you ever tasted, right where later fortunes were taken out in gold at grass roots. Think of it!' Mrs. Womack last week told the following story of how gold came to be discovered in Cripple Creek: 'The

Womacks were always crazy about mining,' she said. 'Samuel Womack, father of Robert and my husband, William, came to Colorado in [the] very early days and engaged in silver mining in Central City. But when he came here he invested in cattle and had the Sun View [sic] ranch, about 14 miles south of Colorado Springs. It was one of the finest ranches. More grazing land was needed for the stock and my husband and I, Bob Womack, their sister, Miss Lida G. Womack, with Emery Lowe, a brother-in-law, went to the site of the Cripple Creek district, where land was preempted, a homestead taken up and cabins built. It was in 1887, I think, that we went there. Bob came and went. He did not pay a great deal of attention either to the mining or the work with the cattle. But my husband had a mine and was much more interested in that than he was in the cattle. He talked of nothing else. He took some ore to Col. Theodore Lowe in Denver to be assayed, but was told it could be only a pocket he might have discovered. After staying up there for about five years my husband and I went to Kentucky. It was while we were there that the exciting discoveries of gold in Cripple Creek were. My husband had said while we were in Kentucky that when we should go back to Colorado he would work his mine some more. They said Bob Womack found gold in Cripple Creek and came to Colorado Springs and told everyone about it. I don't know about that. And I don't know either, anything about whether the ore he discovered was from the mine my husband had worked. I don't say it was. But my husband was the one who discovered gold in Cripple Creek. And he worked hard trying to determine whether there were large deposits of it there. When we came back from from Kentucky he [William] returned to the place, which was then a famous mining camp, to work and try to recover his fortune. But I would not go up there. He wanted me to, but I never would do it. I could not bear to go back there when I thought of what we had lost. Today I look out of a window of my house and see the light of the Rogers shrine on Cheyenne mountain. I see the Myron Stratton home. I see on every hand great things here that were made possible by Cripple Creek gold mining. And then I think of my husband's interest in mining and of how he sought for gold at Cripple Creek, and discovered it, and got no benefit from his discovery. I think of Bob Womack, who for seven years before his death was a helpless paralytic, and of how his sister, Miss Lida Womack, who had a boarding house at St. Vrain street and North Nevada avenue, took care of him, and worked hard to be able to do it, when he had been the one who came down to Colorado Springs and announced the discovery of gold. Can't you see how I have had no desire ever to go to Cripple Creek? But now I don't know but that I shall go up there. My granddaughter writes me the road has been improved and that the trip is an easy one. I suppose I should find the altitude a little high for me now. And so I think when warm weather comes, I may go to Cripple Creek, after all.' William Womack for many years operated the Antlers livery. He was well known in the city, prior to his death which occurred in 1919. Mrs. Womack makes her home with her daughter, Mrs. Jack Edwards. Mr. Edwards is [a] jailer at the county jail. She has two other daughters, Mrs. Homer Davis, who lives in the Black forest, and Mrs. Ella Wasson, who lives in Los Angeles, Calif. It has been said that the gold Robert Womack discovered one day while walking along was from the famous Gold King vein. Bob Womack died in 1911."

Perhaps the interviewer, C. B. Dudley, who wrote the piece, was being kind to the elderly Mrs. Ida Womack. Or, perhaps he was not aware of the true history and facts regarding the first gold discovery in the Cripple Creek area that led to the "Greatest Gold Camp On Earth."

As has been previously pointed out, if in fact, William Womack had discovered gold, a claim was never filed with the El Paso County courthouse. If, for argument's sake, Ida Womack's assertions were true, why did they leave the area and return to Kentucky? Then, once they learned of the Cripple Creek gold rush, as Mrs. Womack recounted, William thought about returning to work his mine again. Yet, the William Womack family did not return to Colorado until 1898, six years after the Cripple Creek gold rush began. Further, it is documented that the family settled in Colorado Springs, not Cripple Creek, where William Womack found employment at the Antlers livery stables.

Possibly due to her age, or perhaps her bitterness, Mrs. Womack's recollection of her own early history, as well as her in-law's history was quite flawed. Ida and her husband, William, settled in at the Welty ranch, which William and Bob had purchased. William and Ida did not "homestead," nor did they build cabins. Nor was it in 1887, as she claimed, for the couple had returned to Kentucky in 1885. Her family history is also flawed. Samuel Redd Womack first mined for silver in Payne's Bar, later, Idaho Springs, not Central City. Margaret Womack was married to Theodore Lowe, not Emery Lowe, Theodore's brother. William Womack died in 1931, not 1919, as that was the death date of his father, Samuel Redd Womack.

Finally, there are many glaring inaccurate accounts made by C. B. Dudley in his account of the history of the Cripple Creek gold strike. Robert "Bob" Womack did not discover gold simply by "walking along." This implies that Bob Womack just happened to be there, when in fact, it was Bob Womack who staked a claim, sunk a shaft, and recorded the claim with the El Paso County courthouse. And as was often misreported in the *Colorado Springs Gazette*, despite the fact that they carried his obituary, Robert "Bob" Miller Womack died on August 10, 1909, not 1911.

Despite all the inaccurate newspaper reporting, and bitter accounts from family members, the history is indisputable.

Bob Womack's legacy will forever remain as the first to discover gold in the Cripple Creek region, launching the last of America's great gold rushes. Because of this discovery, Bob Womack helped create the "Greatest Gold Camp On Earth."

As for Womack's beloved Cripple Creek, the sleepy mountain mining camp saw a rebirth in 1991. When legalized gambling once again became a reality in October of 1991, exactly one hundred years to the month of Bob Womack's gold discovery, many of Cripple Creek's century old buildings were renovated for new use; gambling halls.

Mining has also seen a resurgence in the past few years. However it is corporate mining, not individual. Thus, many of the century old historic mining properties have literally been swallowed up by the advances of new mining technology.

To this day, over a hundred years after Bob Womack discovered gold, and now more commercial than ever, gold is still being mined. There are still stories being told and history being discovered in Bob Womack's Cripple Creek, the Greatest Gold Camp on Earth.

Bob Womack's painting has been in the John Gresham family for decades. Gresham's great grandfather, Roy F. Morton, owned a frame shop in Colorado Springs where painter, Charles Craig, purchased a frame for the painting. (John and Gayle Gresham family collection)

Womack/Wommack Genealogy

The William Womack family emigrated from England, in approximately 1610, settling in America near the TideWater area of what would become Henrico County, Virginia.

The following is part of the Womack/Wommack genealogical line. The extensive line has been simplified to reflect Robert "Bob" Miller Womack's line in relation to the author's line starting with the two brothers John and Daniel that used different spellings to their names.

John W. Womack (1781-1859)
  & Phoebe Boone Bryan (1783-1860)
      Samuel Redd Womack (1819-1919)
       & Corella A. Booker (1821-1879)
         Robert Miller "Bob" Womack (1844-1909) Unmarried

Daniel Wommack (1793-1862)
  & Mary "Polly" Owen (1795-1881)
      James Robert Wommack (1824-)
       & Elizabeth "Polly" Owen (1827-)
      James Robert Wommack (1820-1858)
      & Mary Jane (1824-)
         Robert Jesse Wommack (1855-1934)
         & Eva Elizabeth Wommack (1856-1926)
            Daniel Elbert Wommack (1899-1970)
            & Hazel Mildred Haun (1899-1972)
               Clovis Daniel Wommack (1936-1999)
               & Joyce Darlene Hoglund (1939-2000)
                  Linda Renee Wommack (1958-)

The complete Womack/Wommack family genealogy, compiled over fifty years of research, by my mother, the late Joyce Darlene Hoglund Wommack, is now in the possession of the author.

My mother was invited to provide copies to the Family Genealogical archives in Salt Lake City, Utah, and readily did so. The family genealogy is also available online at the Womack/Wommack web site. In 1997, my mother, Joyce Hoglund Wommack, presented this Womack/Wommack genealogy, in a gold parchment document to the then director of the Cripple Creek District Museum.

One error to be corrected regarding Bob Womack is that he did not come from the Cripple Creek area of Virginia, although there is an area in Virginia of that name and his ancestors did settle in Virginia. An interesting side note, it has been said that the iconic song, "Up on Cripple Creek," by the 1960s group, The Band, was written about Cripple Creek, Colorado. It was not. There are several interviews by various members of the group who have commented on the origins of the song over the years. Robbie Robertson, who wrote the song, said in a 1988 interview with *The Studio* magazine, that the song was written about the area where the band members grew up, the northern area of Virginia where Cripple Creek flows, in Wythe County, Virginia. Further, in an interview with *Time* magazine, dated January 12, 1970, Robertson stated that the Appalachian Mountains of northern Virginia, inspired the musical roots resulting in the iconic tune.

Chapter One Notes

1. The Womack/Wommack Family Genealogical Records, compiled over forty years by my mother, the late Joyce Darlene Hoglund Wommack, are housed in the Family Genealogical Center at Salt Lake City, Utah. The family genealogy is also available on line at the Womack/Wommack website. All land, birth, marriage, death records, and wills obtained by my mother over the years are now in the pocession of the author.

2. The gold discovery at Payne's Bar resulted in the mining town of Idaho Springs.

3. In 1858, William Greenberry Russell found gold at Cherry Creek, not far from where Denver City would eventually be established.

4. Gregory's and Russell's gold find at Gregory Gulch spawned the mining towns of Black Hawk, and just a half mile upstream, Central City. The area became known as the "Richest Square Mile on Earth."

5. Leyendecker, Liston E. The Griffith Family & The Founding of Georgetown, page. 7.

6. History of Clear Creek and Gilpin Counties, page 305. Also see Sprague, Marshall. Money Mountain, page 7.

7. Blevins, Daily, Nicholl, Otto and Sturdevant, Legends & Loves of William Jackson Palmer, page 100.

8. Royem, Robert T. America's Railroad, page 5.

9. Kaelin, Celinda Reynolds. Pikes Peak Backcountry.

10. Drake, Raymond L. and Grimstad, Bill. The Last Gold Rush, page 11.

11. The 7th Annual Report of the Untitled States Geological and Geological Survey of the Territories, 1874. Trachyte is a gray-colored, or lightly colored rock with traces of high grade mineral ore. Sylvanite is often described as "white gold," often containing high traces of gold.

12. Ida Van Dyk was distantly related to both the Womack and Lowe families of Kentucky.

13. A long-held Cripple Creek legend is that the sale of the Welty ranch to the Womacks also included two pigs. See Sprague, Marshall. Money Mountain, page 26. The same legend has often been repeated regarding Bob Womack's sale of the Gold King Mine. There is no substantial evidence for either claim.

14. While there is no public access to Womack's cabin at Poverty Gulch, it can be seen high in the hills above Cripple Creek.

15. The World's Greatest Gold Camp, Volume II, 2010, page 6. Western Museum of Mining and Industry.

16. Wommack, From the Grave.

17. Edward Blair, Leadville: Colorado's Magic City, page 49.

18. Ed Hunter, The World's Greatest Gold Camp, Volume II, 2010. page 10. Western Museum of Mining and Industry.

19. Sprague, Marshall. Money Mountain, page 19.

20. Ed Hunter, The World's Greatest Gold Camp, Volume II, 2010. page 10. Western Museum of Mining and Industry.

21. Sprague, Marshall. Money Mountain, page 28. of the Tutt Library, Colorado College, Colorado Springs, Colorado.

Chapter Two Notes

1. Sprague, Marshall. Money Mountain, page 45. Womack's El Paso Claim should not be confused with the El Paso mine, located much later on Beacon Hill, south of Cripple Creek.

2. Cripple Creek Colorado Commemorative Centennial Program, page 19, Wommack, Linda. "There Had to Be Gold." The $250 1890 figure would be a little over $4,000 in today's figures.

3. El Paso County Court Records, Colorado Springs, Colorado.

4. Spell, Forgotten Men of Cripple Creek, page 41. El Paso County Court Records list the following mining claims as: The Robert E. Lee, located February 20, 1891 by George Carr, William Spell, and M. C. Lankford.

The Blanche, located February 20, 1891 by George Carr, William Spell, and M. C. Lankford. The Hobo, located February 20, 1891 by George Carr, William Spell, and M. C. Lankford.

The Panhandle, located February 20, 1891 by George Carr, William Spell, and M. C. Lankford. The Blue Bell, located February 20, 1891 by George Carr, William Spell, and M. C. Lankford.

5. ibid., pages 39-40.

6. ibid., page 43.

7. ibid., page 53.

8.   ibid.

9.   Howbert, Memories of a Lifetime in the Pike's Peak Region, page 269.

10.   Mazulla, Fred M. Cripple Creek: The First 100 Years, page 14. Spell, Forgotten Men of Cripple Creek, page 41.

11.   Spell, Forgotten Men of Cripple Creek, page 43.

12.   Aldrich, John K., Ghosts of Teller County, page 9.

13.   Levine, Brian, Cities Gold: Victor, Cripple Creek Mining District, page. 8.

14.   Benjamin H. Eaton served as Colorado's governor for one term.

15. El Paso County records, Colorado Springs, Colorado. Also see Spell, Forgotten Men of Cripple Creek, page 49.

16. Waters, Frank, Midas of the Rockies, page 53.

17. Stratton would later become a benefactor and trustee of the school. In 1902, a three-story gray-colored brick building, was erected, known as Stratton Hall.

18. Spell, Forgotten Men of Cripple Creek, page 59.

19. Cripple Creek Colorado Commemorative Centennial Program,

page 37, Levine, Brian. "Billion Dollar Boomtown."

20. Mazulla, Fred M. Cripple Creek: The First 100 Years, page 16.

21. Ed Hunter, The World's Greatest Gold Camp, Volume II, 2010, page 10. Western Museum of Mining and Industry. Howbert, Memories of a Lifetime in the Pike's Peak Region, page 269. Park County, one of the original counties of Colorado Territory, was later divided when Teller County was created from portions of Park County and El Paso County, in 1899. Therefore, Vindicator Mine was located in the original region of Park County.

22. Spell, Forgotten Men of Cripple Creek, page 59. Drake, Raymond L. and Grimstad, Bill. The Last Gold Rush, page 11.

23. Ed Hunter, The World's Greatest Gold Camp, Volume II, 2010, page 10. Western Museum of Mining and Industry.

24. Spell, Forgotten Men of Cripple Creek, page 45.

25. Wommack, Linda, From the Grave.

26. Creek Colorado Commemorative Centennial Program, page 40, Levine, Brian. "Billion Dollar Boomtown."

27. 1893 Cripple Creek Business Directory.

Chapter Three Notes

1. Levine, Brian, Cities Gold: Victor, Cripple Creek Mining District, page. 8.

2. Spell, Forgotten Men of Cripple Creek.

3. ibid.

4. Smith, The Trail of Silver & Gold.

5. Waters, Frank, Midas of the Rockies.

6. The World's Greatest Gold Camp, Volume II, 2010, page 6.

Western Museum of Mining and Industry.

7. Levine, Brian. The Portland: Colorado's Richest Gold Mine.

8. ibid.

9. Spell, Forgotten Men of Cripple Creek.

10. Smith, Duane. Henry M. Teller, Colorado's Grand Old Man.

11. Lamm, Richard and Smith, Duane A. Pioneers & Politicians, pg. 45.

12. Sprague, Money Mountain.

13. Pulcipher, Robert S., Dorsett, Lyle W., and Adams, Eugene H. The Pioneer Western Bank: First of Denver 1860-1980. First Interstate Bank of Denver, 1984.

14. Levine, Brian. The Portland: Colorado's Richest Gold Mine.

15. Cripple Creek Colorado Commemorative Centennial Program, page 37, Levine, Brian. "Billion Dollar Boomtown."

16. Spell, Forgotten Men of Cripple Creek.

17. Feitz, Cripple Creek!

18. Levine, Brian, Cities Gold: Victor, Cripple Creek Mining Dist.

19. Sprague, Money Mountain.

Chapter Four Notes

1. Ed Hunter, The World's Greatest Gold Camp, Volume II, 2010. page 5. Western Museum of Mining and Industry.

2. Feitz, Ghost Towns of the Cripple Creek District, page 35.

3. ibid, page 6. The mining town of Leadville's elevation is 10, 152 feet.

4. Lamm and Smith, Pioneers & Politicians, page 51.

5. ibid., page 51.

6. ibid., page 52.

7. Martin, Corpse On Boomerang Road, page 5.

8. Williams, Cripple Creek Conflagrations, pages 7 and 8.

9. ibid.

10. ibid., page 10.

11. ibid., page 11.

12. ibid.

13. Cripple Creek Morning Times, April 30, 1896.

14. Williams, Cripple Creek Conflagrations, page 25.

15. Levine, Cripple Creek - Victor Mining District, page 27.

16. Wommack, Colorado's Landmark Hotels. The name was changed to the Hotel Imperial in 1917. 17.Wolfe, The Gold Camp Road, page 12.

18 Today, the route of the Colorado Springs & Cripple Creek District Railroad is known as the Gold Camp Road.

19. Levine, Cripple Creek - Victor Mining District, page 10. Also see Paul Morgensen, The Stratton Independence Controversy Revisited, Volume II, 2010, page 58. Western Museum of Mining and Industry. It is interesting to note that, Stratton's attorney, Verner Z. Reed, made a cool million dollars by facilitating the sale.

20. Sprague, The King of Cripple Creek, page 93.

21. Wommack, From the Grave.

22. Spell, Forgotten Men of Cripple Creek, page 130.

23. Martin, Corpse On Boomerang Road, page 194.

24. Spell, Forgotten Men of Cripple Creek, pages 133-135.

25. The Gazette article was incorrect regarding the age of Bob's father. In February of 1908, Samuel Redd Womack was eighty-nine years old. Joyce Womack's genealogical research, Womack/Wommack family genealogy.

26. Womack/Wommack family genealogy, in possession of the author

and also available through the Family Genealogical archives in Salt Lake City, Utah.

27. Here Lies Colorado Springs, Wommack, Linda entry page 177.

28. The Womack family plot is located in Block 19, Lot 2. Wommack, From the Grave.

Bibliography

Primary Sources

Colorado College, Cripple Creek Ledgers. Included in this work are the Cripple Creek Sewerage Company, records from 1902 - 1904. El Paso County Abstract ledgers for the years 1891 through 1896. Anaconda Gold Mining Company stock ledger for the years 1892-1899, company controlled by banker, David H. Moffat.

Cripple Creek District Museum. Cripple Creek Directories, maps and mining records.

Denver Public Library Western History Department.

History of Clear Creek, Boulder and Gilpin Counties. O. L. Baskin & Co. Originally published in 1880, reproduced in 1971.

El Paso County Court Records, Colorado Springs, Colorado.

Womack/Wommack family genealogy, compiled by Joyce Darlene Hoglund Wommack. Family Genealogical archives, Salt Lake City, Utah.

Newspapers

The various newspapers accessed for this work are noted in the text along with the exact quotes.

Archives and Additional Sources

Colorado History Center.

Denver Public Library.

Green County, Missouri, land records, birth and death records.

Tutt Library, Colorado College, Colorado Springs, Colorado.

Pioneer Museum, Colorado Springs, Colorado.

Books

Aldrich, John K., *Ghosts of Teller County*. Centennial Graphics, 1986.

Blair, Edward. *Leadville, Colorado's Magic City*, Pruett Publishing, 1980.

Blevins, Tim, Daily, Dennis, Nicholl, Chris, Otto, Calvin P., and Sturdevant, Katherine S. *Legends & Loves of William Jackson Palmer*. Pikes Peak Library District, 2009.

City of Colorado Springs, *Here Lies Colorado Springs*. Bob Womack entry by Linda Wommack, 1996. Drake, Raymond L. and Grimstad, Bill. *The Last Gold Rush*, Pollux Press, 1983.

Feitz, Leland. *Cripple Creek!* Little London Press, 1967.

Feitz, Leland. *Ghost Towns of the Cripple Creek District*, Little London Press, 1974.

Howbert, Irving. *Memories of a Lifetime in the Pike's Peak Region*. G. P. Putnam's & Sons, 1925. Lamm, Richard and Smith, Duane A. *Pioneers & Politicians*. Pruett Publishing, 1984.

Kaelin, Celinda Reynolds. *Pikes Peak Backcountry*. Caxton Press, 1999.

Levine, Brian, *Cities Gold: Victor, Cripple Creek Mining District*, Century One Press, 1981.

Levine, Brian. *The Portland: Colorado's Richest Gold Mine*. Syzygy Gold Mining Company, 1989. Levine, Brian. *Cripple Creek: City of Influence*, Cripple Creek Historic Preservation Department, 1994. Levine, *Cripple*

Creek - Victor Mining District. Century One Press, 1987.

Leyendecker, Liston E. *The Griffith Family & The Founding of Georgetown*, University of Colorado Press, 2001.

Martin, MaryJoy. *Corpse On Boomerang Road.* Western Reflections Publishing Company, 2004. Mazulla, Fred M. *Cripple Creek: The Fist 100 Years*, A. B. Hirschfeld Press, 1956.

Noel, Thomas J. and Norman, Cathleen M. *A Pikes Peak Partnership: The Penroses and the Tutts.* University Press of Colorado, 2000.

Noel, Thomas J. *Buildings of Colorado.* Oxford University Pres, 1997.

Pulcipher, Robert S., Dorsett, Lyle W., and Adams, Eugene H. *The Pioneer Western Bank: First of Denver 1860-1980.* First Interstate Bank of Denver, 1984.

Royem, Robert T. *America's Railroads*, Durango & Silverton Narrow Gauge Railroad Museum, 2007. Smith, Duane. *Henry M. Teller, Colorado's Grand Old Man.* University Press of Colorado, 2002. Smith, Duane. *Horace Tabor: His Life and his Legend*, Colorado Associated Press, Boulder, Colorado, 1973.

Smith, Duane. *The Trail of Silver & Gold: Mining in Colorado, 1859-2009.* University Press of Colorado, 2009.

Sprague, Marshall. *Money Mountain*, Bison Books, 1953.

Sprague, Marshall. *The King of Cripple Creek.* Friends of the Pikes Peak Library District, 1994.

Spell, Leslie Doyle. *Forgotten Men of Cripple Creek.* Big Mountain Press, 1959.

Waters, Frank, *Midas of the Rockies.* Sage/Swallow Press, 1939.

Williams, Lester L. *Cripple Creek Conflagrations: The Great Fires of 1896 that Burned Cripple Creek, Coloraado.* Filter Press, 1994.

Wommack, Linda. *From the Grave: A Roadside Guide to Colorado's Pioneer Cemeteries.* Caxton Press, Caldwell, Idaho, 1998.

Wommack, Linda. *Colorado's Landmark Hotels*, Filter Press, 2012.

Wommack, Linda. *Our Ladies of the Tenderloin,* Caxton Press, 2005.

Wommack, Linda. *Haunted Cripple Creek & Teller County.* History Press, 2018.

Wolfe, Doris. *The Gold Camp Road: The Short Line to Cripple Creek and Victor.* Self-published, 1988.

Journals, Periodicals, Pamphlets and Magazines

Cripple Creek Colorado Commemorative Centennial Program, City of Cripple Creek, 1991. *There Had to be Gold by* Wommack, Linda.

Here Lies Colorado Springs, Evergreen Cemetery, 1993.

Evergreen Cemetery Walking Tour Guide. Evergreen Cemetery, 1994. Robert Miller Womack information provided by Linda Wommack.

Keske, Maralyn S. *Residents of Sunnyside Cemetery, Victor, Colorado and Fourmile Cemetery, Fourmile Community, Co: 1875 - 1988.* Self-published, 1989.

McMechen, Edgar C. *The Founding of Cripple Creek,* Colorado Magazine, January 1935.

True West Magazine, August 1992. *Bob Womack: A Common Cowpoke Discovers Gold.* By Wommack, Linda.

The World's Greateat Gold Camp Western Museum of Mining and Industry, Volume II, 2010.

About the Author

A Colorado native, Linda Wommack, is a Colorado historian and historical consultant. An award-winning writer, she has written eleven books on Colorado history, including Murder in the Mile High City, Colorado's Landmark Hotels, From the Grave; Colorado's Pioneer Cemeteries, Our Ladies of the Tenderloin; Colorado's Legends in Lace, Colorado History for Kids, Colorado's Historic Mansions and Castles, Ann Bassett, Colorado's Cattle Queen and Haunted History of Cripple Creek and Teller County. She has also contributed to two anthologies concerning Western Americana.

Linda has been a contributing editor for True West Magazine since 1995. She has also been a staff writer, contributing a monthly article for Wild West Magazine, since 2004. She has also written for The Tombstone Epitaph, the nation's oldest continuously published newspaper, since 1993. Linda also writes for several publications throughout her state.

Linda's research has been used in several documentary accounts for the national Wild West History Association, historical treatises of the Sand Creek Massacre, as well as critical historic aspects for the new Lawman & Outlaw Museum in Cripple Creek, Colorado, which opened in 2007.

Linda feeds her passion for history with activities in many local, state, and national preservation projects, participating in historical venues, including speaking engagements, hosting tours, and is involved in historical reenactments across the state.

As a longtime member of the national Western Writers of America, she has served as a judge for the acclaimed national Spur Awards in Western Americana literature for eight years. She is a member of both the state and national Cemetery Preservation Associations, the Gilpin County Historical Society, the national Wild West History Association and an honorary lifetime member of the Pikes Peak Heritage Society. As a member of Women Writing the West, Linda has organized quarterly meetings for the Colorado members of WWW for the past ten years, served on the 2014 WWW Convention Steering Committee, and currently is serving her fourth term as a board member and is the Chair for the DOWNING Journalism Award.

CPSIA information can be obtained
at www.ICGtesting.com
Printed in the USA
FSHW011509051019
62681FS